Diet recommendations for TCM - Bladder - Moisture and cold in the bladder

Please check these recommendations always with a nutrition consultant, therapist, doctor or dietician. The recipes and the list of ingredients are supporting the conventional medical therapy.
The calorie disclosures of fresh ingredients (fruit and vegetables) vary according to quality and time of harvest. The contents were checked by a dietician and a nutrition consultant for the Traditional Chinese Medicine (TCM).

Author:
©2019 Josef Miligui
www.ebns.at

AF220144

Source:
The lists are created from the EBNS database for nutritional counseling. The database is used by dietitians, therapists and doctors for advising the patient / client.

Literature:
The specialist literature and the training documents of the German and Austrian dietary and traditional Chinese medicine serve as a knowledge base. We have used the documents as a basis of knowledge, adapted it to our experience and completed them.
http://di-book.com

Production and publishing:
BoD – Books on Demand, Norderstedt
ISBN: 9783752892475

Diet recommendations for TCM - Bladder - Moisture and cold in the bladder

1 Treatment strategy

Expel cold, dissolve moisture, make waterways consistent. The cold quickly turns into heat.

2 Avoid

n.a.

3 Breakfast

	kkal. per serving
Carrot and rice gruel soup	101
Carrot Risotto	308
Celery juice	33
Fennel-Rice Soup	155
Hearty winter breakfast	678
Hummus (Chickpeasmash)	542
Kuzu soup in the morning	12
Legumes	31
Millet with egg and butter	338
Polenta with ratatouille	225
Pumpkin-yoghurt soup	68
Quinoa piquant with avocado	561
Reissue soup with seaweed	130
Rice congee with carrots and fennel	131
Soup with egg yolk	173
Tea from bearberry leaf	0
Tea from birch leaves	0
Tea from cinnamon sticks	2
Tea from ginseng	1
Tea mixture - reducing uric acid	0
Thick pea soup	123

4 Snack

5 Lunch

6 Afternoon

7 Dinner

8 Any time

9   Recipes

(rec.) = You can use more.
(little) = You should use less than specified
(no) omit.

9.1   8 treasures of rice

Strengthens kidney and bladder, builds up Qi, strengthens the spleen, repels moisture, reduces internal heat, prevents cancer, builds heart, calms nerves.
Cooking time approx. 1 hour
Calories p. portion: 223
4 portions

Quantity of ingredients:
Lily bulbs 1 table spoon / 5g. () - cool - sweet, bitter .... *
Longane 1 table spoon / 5g. (yes) - warm - sweet .... *
King Solomon's-seal 1 table spoon / 5g. (yes) - neutral - sweet, bitter............. *
Yam root, yam root tuber 1 table spoon / 5g. (rec.) - neutral - sweet .... *
Coix (seeds) YiYi Ren 1 table spoon / 5g. (little) - cool - sweet, neutral........... *
Rice wild (nature rice) 1 1/2 cups / 240g. (rec.) - neutral - sweet, bitter .... metal
Water 8-10 cups / 800g. (yes) - cool - salty...earth

Cooking instructions:
Each one 1 tbsp: Bai He, Longan, Yu Zhu, Da Zao, Shan Yao, Lian Mi, Yi Yi Ren, Qian Shi
Add hot water and soak for about 30 minutes. Then add 1 - 2 cups of rice (normal) and simmer for 1/2 to 1 hour until the rice is very soft. Or: Cook for about 3 hours with the herbs a congee. Then the herbs do not have to be soaked.

9.2   Artichoke soup

Cools heat, nourishes heart, stomach and lungs Yin.
Cooking time approx. 40 min
Calories p. portion: 142
3 portions
Allergens: GLN

Quantity of ingredients:
Artichoke 4 pieces / 400g. (rec.) - cool - sweet, bitter ....fire
Butter organic 1 table spoon / 20g. (little) - neutral - sweet ....earth
Onion (shallot) 1 piece / 20g. (yes) - warm - acrid, sweet .... metal
Corn flour 1 table spoon / 10g. (little) - neutral - sweet...............................earth

Nutmeg 1 pinch / 0,5g. (rec.) - warm - acrid .... metal
Basic recipe for a vegetable soup (nutritious) 1 cup / 250g. (rec.) - neutral - *. *
Salt 1 pinch / 0,5g. (little) - cold - salty .... water
Lemon 1/4 piece / 8g. (omit) - cold - sour .... wood
Lemon peel 1/4 piece / 1g. (yes) - cool - bitter .... fire
Turmeric (yellow root) 1 pinch / 1g. (yes) - warm - bitter .... *
Sesame, white 1 teaspoon / 10g. (yes) - neutral - sweet .... earth

Cooking instructions:
Boil the artichokes in 2 liters of water with salt until the outer leaves are light removable. Remove leaves and flower center (fibrous) so that only the soil remains.
Melt the butter, cut the onion into small pieces and steam gently; add some cornmeal, nutmeg; brew with vegetable soup; add salt, a little lemon peel and juice, turmeric and artichoke bottoms, cook gently and puree; Season with Tahin and sprinkle with sesame before serving.

9.3   Basic recipe for a beef broth (clear)

Strengthens Qi and Yang, is very warming.
Cooking time approx. 4-8 hours
Calories p. portion: 114
10 portions
Allergens: O

Quantity of ingredients:
Beef soup meat 1,1 lbs / 500g. (little) - warm - sweet .... earth
Beef meatbones 5/8 oz / 200g. (little) - warm - sweet .... earth
Vinegar (Red wine vinegar) 1 dash / 3g. (little) - warm - sour, bitter .... wood
Juniper berry 8 pieces / 6g. (rec.) - warm - sweet, acrid, bitter..................... fire
Rosemary 1 pinch / 1g. (yes) - warm - bitter .... fire
Carrot 3 pieces / 210g. (yes) - neutral - sweet .... earth
Parsnip 2 pieces / 300g. (rec.) - cool - bitter... fire
Leek 1 piece / 200g. (yes) - warm - acrid ... . metal
Ginger fresh 1/2 teaspoon / 5g. (rec.) - warm - acrid................................. metal
Lovage 1 stem / 15g. (yes) - warm - acrid, bitter .... metal
Lovage 1 stem / 15g. (yes) - warm - acrid, bitter .... metal
Clove 2 pieces / 2g. (yes) - warm - acrid.... .... metal
Pimento 6 pieces / 12g. (yes) - hot - acrid.. .... metal
Anise (Common Fennel) 2 pieces / 1g. (yes) - warm - acrid .... earth
Salt 1 teaspoon / 5g. (little) - cold - salty .... water
Water 3,3 lbs / 1300g. (yes) - cool - salty... .... earth

Cooking instructions:
Heat water, a dash of red wine vinegar, some juniper berries, a little rosemary, bones and meat till it boils; add carrot, parsnip, leek, ginger, lovage, clove, allspice, star anise and a little salt; simmer for 4-8 hours then strain.
Refrigerate for later use.

9.4   Basic recipe for a chicken broth worming

Strengthens Qi and blood, is very warm.
Cooking time approx. 2-3 hours
Calories p. portion: 90
9 portions
Allergens: L

Quantity of ingredients:
Chicken meat 1/2 piece / 600g. (rec.) - warm - sweet .... wood
Carrot 2 pieces / 150g. (yes) - neutral - sweet .... earth
Leek 1 stick / 45g. (yes) - warm - acrid .... metal
Celery root 1 piece / 500g. (little) - cool - sweet .... earth
Ginger fresh 2 slices / 2g. (rec.) - warm - acrid .... metal
Juniper berry 1 teaspoon / 3g. (rec.) - warm - sweet, acrid, bitter .... fire
Bay leaf 3 pieces / 2g. (yes) - warm - acrid .... metal
Water 4 cup / 900g. (yes) - cool - salty .... earth

Cooking instructions:
Remove chicken parts from fat. Place chicken pieces in a saucepan with hot water and heat till it boils briefly, skimming any resulting foam. Add coarsely chopped vegetables and all spices and cook over medium heat for 2 to 3 hours. Strain the finished soup. Throw away vegetables and bones.
Tip: If you want to use the meat as a soup insert, take out after 45 minutes and return only the bones in the soup.
Refrigerate for later use.

9.5   Basic recipe for a reissue soup (Congee)

Warms the stomach and spleen, harmonizes the intestine, forces Qi, reduces moisture.
Cooking time approx. 2-4 hours
Calories p. portion: 140
3 portions

Quantity of ingredients:

Rice variety any 1 cup / 120g. (little) - warm - sweet .... metal
Water 6 cups / 700g. (yes) - cool - salty ....earth

Cooking instructions:

Cook rice and water in a ratio of about 1: 6. The amount of water
determines the thickness of the mash (matter of taste).
Put the rice in a saucepan with a heavy lid. It is important to simmer the
rice after a short boil on the slightest flame, otherwise it burns.
Boil the rice for 2-4 hours. The longer it cooks, the more it strengthens.
If you want to eat the dish for breakfast, you can put the rice on just
before bedtime.
To be on the safe side, you should first check the behavior of your pot
and cooker under observation for a similar amount of time, so that
nothing burns.
Refrigerate for later use.

9.6   Basic recipe for a vegetable soup, nutritious

Strengthens spleen and lung, regulates Qi flow, builds up Qi, dries out,
passes downwardly, strengthens stomach Qi.
Cooking time approx. 2-3 hours
Calories p. portion: 48
5 portions
Allergens: L

Quantity of ingredients:

Olive oil 1 table spoon / 4g. (rec.) - cool - sweet ....earth
Onion white 1 piece / 60g. (yes) - warm - acrid .... metal
Carrot 3 pieces / 200g. (yes) - neutral - sweet ....earth
Parsnip 3/8 lbs - 6oz / 150g. (rec.) - cool - bitter ....fire
Celery root 1 cup / 100g. (little) - cool - sweet...earth
Ginger fresh 1/2 teaspoon / 2g. (rec.) - warm - acrid................................ metal
Lemon 1/2 piece / 25g. (omit) - cold - sour. .... wood
Juniper berry 6 pieces / 6g. (rec.) - warm - sweet, acrid, bitter.....................fire
Thyme dried 1 pinch / 1g. (yes) - warm - bitter... metal
Lovage 1 table spoon / 3g. (yes) - warm - acrid, bitter .... metal
Bay leaf 2 leaves / 1g. (yes) - warm - acrid .... metal
Salt 1 pinch / 1g. (little) - cold - salty .... water
Water 3 cups / 650g. (yes) - cool - salty...earth

Cooking instructions:

Cut the vegetables into cubes.
Heat oil in hot pot, fry shortly onions and vegetables.
Add cold water, then add ginger, bay leaf and lemon juice.

Season with juniper, thyme and lovage. Cover for 2 - 3 hours on a low heat and simmer.
The used vegetables should be thrown away.
The basic recipe serves as a soup base and to refine vegetables, legumes or cereals.
If you want to eat vegetable soup immediately, add the desired vegetables half an hour before.
Refrigerate for later use.

9.7 Beef soup with carrots, leeks, bay leaves

Strengthens spleen Qi, strengthens blood and Qi, moisturizes, relaxes, builds up Qi, spreads, strengthens spleen and liver, regulates Qi flow, strengthens stomach Qi.
Cooking time approx. 2-3 hours
Calories p. portion: 194
5 portions

Quantity of ingredients:
Beef meat 1 lbs / 500g. (little) - warm - sweet ....earth
Carrot 2 pieces / 200g. (yes) - neutral - sweet ....earth
Leek 1/2 piece / 150g. (yes) - warm - acrid ....metal
Bay leaf 3 leaves / 1g. (yes) - warm - acrid ....metal
Corn Grease (Polenta) 1 table spoon / 10g. (little) - neutral - sweet ....earth
Water 2 cup / 450g. (yes) - cool - salty..earth
Salt 1 pinch / 0,5g. (little) - cold - salty ....water

Cooking instructions:
In a saucepan with water (enough to cover the meat), add beef soup meat or leg slice and simmer for a moment; then pour off the broth, rinse the meat with hot water (this will save you from foaming), clean the pot and put the meat in hot water again; add chopped carrot, leek, corn and bay leaf; simmer until the meat is cooked.

9.8 Beluga lentil stew with vegetables

Tonifies Qi and blood, forces kidneys and spleen, dissipates heat and moisture.
Cooking time approx. 20 min
Calories p. portion: 201
5 portions

Quantity of ingredients:

Lentils 1 1/2 cups / 240g. (yes) - neutral - sweet, sour .... water
Water 4-5 cups / 500g. (yes) - cool - salty .... earth
Carrot 3 pieces / 150g. (yes) - neutral - sweet .... earth
Leek 1 piece / 300g. (yes) - warm - acrid .... metal
Kohlrabi 1/2 piece / 200g. (yes) - neutral - acrid, sweet .... earth
Tomato 2 pieces / 80g. (little) - cold - sweet-sour..................................... wood
Onion white 1 piece / 50g. (yes) - warm - acrid .... metal
Bay leaf 2 leaves / 1g. (yes) - warm - acrid .... metal
Fennel 1 piece / 250g. (little) - warm - sweet, little acrid............................. earth
Star anise 2 pieces / 1g. (yes) - hot - acrid.. metal
Juniper berry 6 pieces / 2g. (rec.) - warm - sweet, acrid, bitter..................... fire
Chili (pod or ground) 1 pinch / 0,2g. (yes) - hot - acrid .... metal
Olive oil 3 table spoons / 30g. (rec.) - cool - sweet. .... earth
Salt 1 pinch / 1g. (little) - cold - salty .... water
Ginger fresh 1/2 teaspoon / 2g. (rec.) - warm - acrid................................. metal
Black caraway 1 pinch / 1g. (yes) - warm - acrid, sweet.................................. *

Cooking instructions:

Heat oil in hot pot. Fry onions and add diced vegetables and spices, lentils (washed well) and salt. Cover with cold water (3 fingers wide) and cook for 20 minutes on a low heat.
Sprinkle with fresh herbs and black cumin
Goes well with rice!

9.9 Black-eyed beans stew

Strengthens spleen and kidney, is very nutritious, warms the stomach and spleen, harmonizes the intestine, forces Qi, strengthens stomach and kidney, strengthens spleen and kidney.
Cooking time approx. 20 min
Calories p. portion: 140
5 portions

Quantity of ingredients:

Black-eyed peas 1 cup / 100g. (yes) - neutral - sweet, acrid..................... water
Rice variety any 1 1/2 cups / 200g. (little) - warm - sweet .... metal
Water 10 cups / 1000g. (yes) - cool - salty............. .... earth

Cooking instructions:

Soak the beans overnight and strain.
In a ratio of 1: 2, simmer the beans together with the rice in the Water. Depending on how hot the flame is and how thin the dish should be, more water must be added. Variation: Add vegetables fried in oil, such as carrots, celery tubers, onions or leeks.

9.10 Boiled fillet with potatoebiscuits (Austrian Tafelspitz)

Strengthens spleen Qi, strengthens blood and Qi, moisturizes, relaxes, builds up Qi, spreads, forces Qi, forces spleen, relieves inflammation, moisturizes.
Cooking time approx. 3 hours
Calories p. portion: 454
8 portions
Allergens: L

Quantity of ingredients:
Onion white 1 piece / 50g. (yes) - warm - acrid .... metal
Corn germ oil 1 table spoon / 10g. (little) - neutral - sweet .... earth
Water 32 cup - 1 gallon / 0g. (yes) - cool - salty .... earth
Beef meat 5,4 lbs - 70oz cap of rump / 1800g. (little) - warm - sweet .... earth
Beef meatbones 4n slices with bone marrow / 0g. (little) - warm - sweet ... earth
Salt 1 pinch / 0,5g. (little) - cold - salty .... water
Peppercorns 15 pieces / 0g. (little) - warm - acrid .... metal
Parsnip 1 piece / 0g. (rec.) - cool - bitter .... fire
Carrot 2 pieces / 0g. (yes) - neutral - sweet .... earth
Celery root 1 slice / 0g. (little) - cool - sweet .... earth
Parsley root 2 pieces / 0g. (yes) - cool - sweet .... earth
Leek 1/2 stick / 0g. (yes) - warm - acrid .... metal
Chives 1 table spoon (chopped) / 7g. (yes) - warm - acrid .... metal
Potato 2,2 lbs / 1000g. (yes) - neutral - sweet .... earth
Sunflower oil 2 table spoons / 20g. (little) - cool - sweet .... earth
Salt 1 pinch / 0,5g. (little) - cold - salty .... water

Cooking instructions:
Halve the onions, but do not peel. Brown onions in a pan with fat on the cut surfaces very dark. Wash meat and bones briefly with warm water, drain.
Heat the water till it boils, put in meat and cook gently. Always scoop up rising foam. As soon as no more foam rises, add peppercorns and the onion. Clean and cut root and leeks and add after about two and a half hours cooking time. Simmer for another half hour.
Remove boiled beef from the soup, pour through a sieve and season with salt. Cut roots into bite-sized pieces. Add the soup together with the marrow bones and leave it under the boiling point. Cut the boiled beef into finger-thick slices against the grain, place in the soup, heat again, sprinkle with a little chives.
In addition, cook and peel the potatoes in salted water. Stomp roughly or cut finely. Fry in a pan with the oil crispy.

9.11 Carrot and rice gruel soup

Warms the stomach and spleen, harmonizes the intestine, forces Qi, reduces moisture, strengthens spleen and liver, regulates Qi flow, moisturizes, relaxes, builds up Qi, spreads.
Cooking time approx. 10 min
Calories p. portion: 101
1 portion

Quantity of ingredients:

Basic recipe for a rice soup (Congee) 1 cup / 120g (yes) - neutral - sweet..... *
Carrot 2 pieces / 100g. (yes) - neutral - sweet ....earth
Salt 1 teaspoon / 4g. (little) - cold - salty ....water

Cooking instructions:

Peel and grate carrots. Heat the rice soup (according to the basic recipe) till it boils and add the grated carrots and salt. Cook for 10 minutes.

9.12 Carrot Risotto

Forces stomach, spleen and liver, regulates Qi flow, relaxes, builds up Qi, spreads, dries out, passes downwardly, strengthens stomach Qi, nourishes blood and liver, harmonizes liver and spleen, forces eyesight, preserves the fluids, contracts.
Cooking time approx. 45 min
Calories p. portion: 308
2 portions
Allergens: GL

Quantity of ingredients:

Olive oil 1/2 teaspoon / 5g. (rec.) - cool - sweet ....earth
Onion (spring onion) 2 table spoons / 7g. (yes) - warm - acrid.................metal
Nutmeg 1 pinch / 0,3g. (rec.) - warm - acrid...metal
Parsley 1/2 bunch / 25g. (yes) - warm - bitter...wood
Rice variety any 1/4 lbs - 4oz / 100g. (little) - warm – sweet ....metal
Carrot 5/8 lbs - 8oz / 250g. (yes) - neutral - sweet ....earth
Basic recipe for a vegetable soup (nutritious) 1 cup / 280g. (rec.) - neutral - *. *
Basil (fresh) 1/2 teaspoon / 2g. (rec.) - warm - acric, bitter ....metal
Salt 1 pinch / 1g. (little) - cold - salty ....water
Pepper (ground) 1 pinch / 0,3g. () - warm - acrid ....metal

Cooking instructions:

Heat the oil in a pan, fry the onions in a glassy and very soft manner.
Add parsley, sauté briefly. Add rice, carrots and nutmeg, sauté briefly

while stirring. Add the vegetable stock, season with fennel and basil, heat till it boils and cook for about 20 minutes until the rice and carrots are well. Stir from time to time and add some vegetable stock if necessary. The risotto should be slightly soupy. Just before the end of the cooking time mix in the white wine and simmer the risotto for a short while. Remove risotto from the heat, mix in Parmesan.

9.13 Celery juice

Strengthens stomach Qi, moisturizes, relaxes, builds up Qi, spreads.
Cooking time approx. 5 min
Calories p. portion: 33
1 portion
Allergens: L

Quantity of ingredients:
Celery root 1/2 piece / 200g. (little) - cool - sweet ....earth
Water 1 cup / 120g. (yes) - cool - salty..earth
Salt 1 pinch / 0,5g. (little) - cold - salty ....water

Cooking instructions:
Peel celeriac and cut into pieces and juice. Mix with water and salt as needed.

9.14 Chicken in an Italian style

Forces Qi, blood and Jing, middle heater, builds up spleen and stomach, nourishes Qi, forces essence, preserves the fluids, moisturizes.
Cooking time approx. 1 hour
Calories p. portion: 410
4 portions
Allergens: M

Quantity of ingredients:
Olive oil 3 table spoons / 30g. (rec.) - cool - sweet.....................................earth
Chicken meat 1 piece (cut into 8 pieces) / 700g. (rec.) - warm - sweet..... wood
Garlic 3 cloves / 5g. (rec.) - hot - acrid .... metal
Rosemary 1/2 teaspoon / 2g. (yes) - warm - bitter ....fire
Salt 1 pinch / 1g. (little) - cold - salty .... water
Pepper (ground) 1 pinch / 0,5g. () - warm - acrid .... metal
Water 1 cup / 20g. (yes) - cool - salty...earth
Rice Basmati 1 cup / 120g. (little) - neutral - sweet.................................. metal
Water 6 cups / 400g. (yes) - cool - salty..earth
Salt 1 pinch / 1g. (little) - cold - salty .... water

Lettuce 1 piece / 300g. (little) - cool - sweet, bitter...fire
Olive oil 2 table spoons / 20g. (rec.) - cool - sweet...................................earth
Lemon juice 1/4 piece / 7g. (omit) - cold - sour .... wood
Salt 1 pinch / 1g. (little) - cold - salty .... water
Honey 1 pinch / 2g. (omit) - cold - sweet.... ....earth

Cooking instructions:

In a heavy pan (with lid) heat 1 tbsp of olive oil at low temperature. Add the chicken pieces and fry for a few minutes. Once they start to take on color, add the remaining 2 tablespoons of olive oil and garlic. Turn the chicken parts in the oil and sprinkle with rosemary, salt and pepper. Pour with a little water and heat till it boils. Reduce the heat, put on the lid and stew the chicken for 35 to 45 minutes.

In between, check again and again whether there is enough cooking water, and if necessary, add 1 to 2 tablespoons of water each time.

As soon as the meat comes off the bone, spread the chicken parts on the plates, deglaze the roast residue in the braised pan with a few tablespoons of water or wine and spread over the meat as a sauce.
In the meantime, cook the rice in a saucepan with (1:6) salted water, on a low heat.
Wash and spin the lettuce, finely chop and serve in a bowl. In a small bowl, mix the olive oil, lemon juice, mustard, salt and honey well and add to the salad and add it to the salad.

9.15 Chicken soup with angelica root and buckthorn fruit

Strengthens spleen and nourishes the blood and Yin of the liver, forces Qi and blood, is very warming.
Cooking time approx. 1 1/2 hours
Calories p. portion: 77
3 portions
Allergens: LO

Quantity of ingredients:

Basic recipe for a chicken soup (warming) 2 cup / 500g. (rec.) - warm - * .... *
Bocksdorn fruits (Lycii, goji berry dried 1/8 lbs - 2oz / 50g. (yes) - cool - . wood

Cooking instructions:

When you cook chicken broth according to basic recipes add angelica root and willowberry fruits in the last 40 minutes.
Ingestion: Drink 2-3 cups of broth daily

9.16 Classic ginger chicken with rice wine

warming and nourishing, directs the Qi upwards, forces the libido, against Qi- und Yang-weakness of spleen, heart and kidneys, in lung Qi deficiency, moisture, sensitivity to cold, listlessness.
Cooking time approx. 30 min
Calories p. portion: 357
4 portions
Allergens: GO

Quantity of ingredients:
Butter organic 3 table spoons / 30g. (little) - neutral - sweet ....earth
Ginger fresh 2 table spoons / 18g. (rec.) - warm - acrid ....metal
Salt 1 pinch / 0,5g. (little) - cold - salty ....water
Chicken meat 2 pieces (legs) / 500g. (rec.) - warm - sweet ....wood
Lychee liqueur 1 dash / 2g. (omit) - cool - sweet, sour..................................fire
Curry 1 pinch / 1g. (yes) - warm - acrid ....metal
Sake 1 dash / 1g. (omit) - warm - sweet, bitter, acrid ....metal
Corn 4 table spoons / 30g. (little) - neutral - sweet....................................earth
Millet 1/2 cup / 50g. (yes) - cool - sweet, salty...earth
Water 1 1/2 cups / 200g. (yes) - cool - salty...earth
Salt 1 pinch / 0,5g. (little) - cold - salty ....water
Lettuce 1/2 piece / 100g. (little) - cool - sweet, bitter ....fire
Olive oil 1 table spoon / 10g. (rec.) - cool - sweet ....earth
Vinegar (Apple vinegar) 1 teaspoon / 3g. (little) - warm - sour, bitter .... wood
Water 2 table spoons / 20g. (yes) - cool - salty ....earth
Salt 1 pinch / 0,5g. (little) - cold - salty ....water

Cooking instructions:
Heat butter in a hot pan (preferably made of cast iron or enamel); sauté chopped ginger (about 1 heaped tablespoons per chicken leg) on low heat; add some salt, chicken and/or other parts of the chicken and roast all around with gentle heat; add Lychee liqueur or maple syrup, add a little curry and fry for a short time; stir in plenty of sake; add corn kernels (from the glass, health food trade); boil all the ingredients in the sauce for a few minutes,
until the meat is cooked; season with salt.

This fits: millet, lettuce or lettuce.

9.17 Clear soup from goose

Forces spleen, stomach and lungs, relieves weakness, forces Qi, calms the stomach, gets Qi moving, directs upwards, strengthens spleen and liver, regulates Qi flow, moisturizes, relaxes, builds up Qi, spreads.
Cooking time approx. 2-3 hours
Calories p. portion: 334
6 portions

Quantity of ingredients:
Goose parts 1,1 lbs / 500g. (yes) - neutral - sweet. .... metal
Carrot 1 piece / 100g. (yes) - neutral - sweet .... earth
Onion (shallot) 1 piece / 25g. (yes) - warm - acrid, sweet .... metal
Leek 1 piece / 250g. (yes) - warm - acrid .... metal
Parsley 1 Twig / 4g. (yes) - warm - bitter............... .... wood
Lovage 1 Twig / 4g. (yes) - warm - acrid, bitter .... metal
Water 4 cup / 1000g. (yes) - cool - salty................ .... earth
Salt 1 pinch / 0,5g. (little) - cold - salty .... water

Cooking instructions:
Simmer goose pieces with vegetables and herbs for 2-3 hours. Sift through a fine cloth and cool. Degrease and store in the refrigerator.

9.18 Fennel-Rice Soup

Regulates Qi, warms the inside, lowers cold, forces stomach, relieves constipation, forces Yang, dissolves mucus, reduces wind, spreads, strengthens Qi and kidney Jing, builds up Qi.
Cooking time approx. 15-20 min
Calories p. portion: 156
2 portions
Allergens: EG

Quantity of ingredients:
Basic recipe for a rice soup (Congee) 1 cup / 300g. (yes) - neutral - sweet..... *
Fennel 1/2 piece / 150g. (little) - warm - sweet, little acrid......................... earth
Butter organic 1 table spoon / 15g. (little) - neutral - sweet .... earth
Soy sauce 1 dash / 3g. (little) - cold - salty................. .... water

Cooking instructions:
Cook the fennel softly in the rice soup according to the basic recipe. Before serving, add a piece of butter and some soy sauce.

9.19 Grilled lamb chops with sweetpotatorpuree

Strengthens spleen and kidney Yang, forces Qi, heats middle and lower heater, builds up heart and veins, moisturizes respiratory tract, promotes stomach-spleen harmony.
Cooking time approx. 45 min
Calories p. portion: 914
2 portions
Allergens: E

Quantity of ingredients:
Lamb meat 6 pieces (chops) / 300g. (little) - warm - sweet............................fire
Garlic 2 cloves / 3g. (rec.) - hot - acrid ....metal
Rosemary 2 table spoons / 5g. (yes) - warm - bitter.....................................fire
Salt 1 pinch / 1g. (little) - cold - salty ....water
Olive oil 2 table spoons / 20g. (rec.) - cool - sweet.....................................earth
Sweet potato 3/4 lbs / 300g. (yes) - warm - sweet ....earth
Basil 1 table spoon / 3g. (rec.) - warm - acrid, bitter.....................................fire
Soybean milk 1/4 lbs - 4oz / 100g. (yes) - cool - sweet ....earth
Salt 1 pinch / 1g. (little) - cold - salty ....water
Nutmeg 1 pinch / 0,5g. (rec.) - warm - acrid...metal
Pepper (ground) 1 pinch / 0,5g. () - warm - acrid ....metal
Chard 2 handful / 20g. (little) - cool - bitter, sweet.....................................earth
Spinach 2 handful / 20g. (yes) - cool - sweet, rough ....earth
Savoy cabbage / kale 2 handful / 20g. (yes) - neutral - sweet....................earth
White cabbage 2 handful / 20g. (yes) - neutral - sweet ....earth
Olive oil 2 table spoons / 20g. (rec.) - cool - sweet.....................................earth
Salt 1 pinch / 1g. (little) - cold - salty ....water
Pepper (ground) 1 pinch / 0,5g. () - warm - acrid ....metal

Cooking instructions:
Lamb chops:
Preheat the oven grill to about 180°C/365°F and set the shelf to a height, such that the chops are about 8 to 12 centimeters from the heat source. Remove the fattest of the chops and place them in a fireproof mold. Rub the meat first with garlic, then with the rosemary salt mixture and spread a few teaspoons of olive oil over it.
Turn the lamb chops once so that they are covered with oil on both sides, put them under the grill and grill on both sides for 5 to 7 minutes or until the meat is well browned.

Mashed sweet potatoes:
Peel all sweet potatoes and cut into large cubes, boil gently in salted water and strain. Leave to soak in the 100°C/212°F hot brook for a few minutes. Remove the basil leaves. Puree sweet potatoes.

Approximately Boil 1/8 l soymilk with basil once, then strain a little and strain and mix with the passed sweet potatoes. Season with salt, pepper and nutmeg. Depending on the consistency of the puree, add a little more milk.
Steamed leafy vegetables:
After the season chard, spinach, savoy cabbage, white cabbage, fresh herbs and the mugwort in a pot with olive oil softly. Season with salt and pepper

9.20 Hearty winter breakfast

Forces Qi and Yang, strengthens the body's defenses and warms up, helps with Qi and Yang emptiness.
Cooking time approx. 20 min
Calories p. portion: 678
1 portion
Allergens: ACEG

Quantity of ingredients:

Oat meal 1 cup / 120g. (little) - warm - sweet .... metal
Ginger fresh 1/2 teaspoon / 1g. (rec.) - warm - acrid .... metal
Salt 1 pinch / 1g. (little) - cold - salty .... water
Onion (spring onion) 2 pieces / 40g. (yes) - warm - acrid .... metal
Chicken egg 1 piece / 55g. (little) - neutral - sweet .... earth
Butter organic 1 table spoon / 15g. (little) - neutral - sweet .... earth
Soy sauce 1 dash / 3g. (little) - cold - salty .... water

Cooking instructions:

Soak oatmeal overnight. Boil in the morning with a little ginger, salt and a spring onion or leek and then let it swell until the porridge is soft. Before serving, add a whole egg to the porridge, add the butter and season to taste with a little soy sauce.
Recommendation: Especially suitable for the cold season.

9.21 Hummus (Chickpeasmash)

Strengthens spleen and heart, softens, passes downwardly, moisturizes, relaxes, builds up Qi, spreads, nourishes blood, nourishes blood and liver, harmonizes liver and spleen, forces eyesight, preserves the fluids, contracts.
Cooking time approx. 2 hours
Calories p. portion: 542
2 portions
Allergens: N

Quantity of ingredients:

Chickpeas 1 1/2 cups / 240g. (yes) - cool - sweet, salty............................ water
Wakame 1 teaspoon (grated) / 2g. (little) - cold - salty .... water
Ginger fresh 1/4 teaspoon / 1g. (rec.) - warm - acrid................................ metal
Rosemary 1 pinch / 0,5g. (yes) - warm - bitter ....fire
Olive oil 2 table spoons / 20g. (rec.) - cool - sweet....................................earth
Lemon juice 1 splash / 2g. (omit) - cold - sour.. wood
Water upon need / 0g. (yes) - cool - salty...earth
Garlic 1 clove (scraped) / 2g. (rec.) - hot - acrid .... metal
Parsley 1 teaspoon (chopped) / 2g. (yes) - warm - bitter .... wood
Peppers 1 pinch / 0,2g. (little) - cool - sweet ....earth
Turmeric (yellow root) 1 pinch / 0,2g. (yes) - warm - bitter .... *
Coriander 1 pinch / 0,2g. (yes) - warm - acrid .... metal
Cardamom 1 pinch / 0,2g. (little) - warm - acrid .... metal
Chili (pod or ground) 1 pinch / 0,2g. (yes) - hot - acrid .... metal
Pepper (ground) 1 pinch / 0,2g. () - warm - acrid .... metal

Cooking instructions:

Soak chickpeas overnight or for at least 6 hours, pour off soaking water, boil in fresh water for about 1 to 1 ½ hours with a little seaweed and ginger, allow to cool.
Seasoning with a few splashes of lemon juice and parsley.
Add the pepper, garlic cut into small pieces or pressed, more or less coriander and cardamom powder, little chili powder as desired, Tahin and olive oil.

Puree all ingredients together. Depending on the consistency, add water. It should be a smooth paste.
Spread on cereal, crackers or toasted bread or enjoy with salad.

9.22 Indian Dal soup

Reduces internal heat and moisture, softens, passes downwardly, strengthens spleen and liver, regulates Qi flow, moisturizes, relaxes, builds up Qi, spreads, forces liver and kidney, reduces damp heat.
Cooking time approx. 30 min
Calories p. portion: 256
2 portions
Allergens: EN

Quantity of ingredients:

Lentils 3/8 lbs - 6oz / 175g. (yes) - neutral - sweet, sour............................ water
Sesame oil 3 table spoons / 30g. (yes) - cool - sweet ....earth
Carrot 1 piece / 100g. (yes) - neutral - sweet ....earth

Onion (shallot) 1 piece / 15g. (yes) - warm - acrid, sweet .... metal
Water 1 1/2 cups / 200g. (yes) - cool - salty .... earth
Ginger fresh 2 slices / 1g. (rec.) - warm - acrid .... metal
Salt 1 pinch / 0,5g. (little) - cold - salty .... water
Soy sauce 1 teaspoon / 3g. (little) - cold - salty .... water
Parsley 1 teaspoon (chopped) / 3g. (yes) - warm - bitter .... wood
Thyme 1 teaspoon / 3g. (rec.) - warm - bitter .... *
Basil 1 table spoon / 5g. (rec.) - warm - acrid, bitter .... fire

Cooking instructions:
Soak the lentils overnight.
in a hot pot, carrot, onion and a little ginger fry, pour water. Add the
lentils and cook until soft. Add salt or soy sauce and cook for another 10
minutes.
Stir in parsley before serving; Sprinkle thyme or basil over it.
Variant: Other herbs such as sage, rosemary or lovage allow a variety
of flavors.

9.23 Italian Vegetable and Bean Soup

Moisturizes skin, diuretic, strengthens stomach Qi, moisturizes, relaxes,
builds up Qi, nourishes liver-Yin, cools
heat, produces humors, strengthens spleen and liver, regulates Qi flow,
moisturizes, relaxes, builds up Qi, spreads.
Cooking time approx. 1 hour
Calories p. portion: 204
4 portions
Allergens: L

Quantity of ingredients:
Butter beans white 5/8 oz / 200g. (yes) - neutral - sweet .... water
Onion (shallot) 1 piece / 20g. (yes) - warm - acrid, sweet .... metal
Carrot 1 piece / 70g. (yes) - neutral - sweet .... earth
Olive oil 2 table spoons / 20g. (rec.) - cool - sweet .... earth
Tomato 2 pieces / 80g. (little) - cold - sweet-sour .... wood
Celery root 1/4 lbs / 100g. (little) - cool - sweet .... earth
White cabbage 0,2 lbs / 70g. (yes) - neutral - sweet .... earth
Endive salad 1/8 lbs - 2oz / 50g. (yes) - neutral - bitter .... fire
Salt 1 pinch / 1g. (little) - cold - salty .... water
Pepper (ground) 1 pinch / 0,2g. () - warm - acrid .... metal
Water 2 cup / 450g. (yes) - cool - salty .... earth

Cooking instructions:
Soak beans and cook for 1/2 hour.
Fry onions, carrots and celery in frying oil.
Add tomatoes and water and simmer for 30 minutes.
Cut white cabbage into strips. Add the cabbage and endive salad and
the boiled beans, and season with salt, pepper and olive oil.

9.24 Japanese algae soup

Strengthens spleen and liver, regulates Qi flow, moisturizes, relaxes,
builds up Qi, spreads, nourishes the lungs
and spleen, distributes mucus, dissolves mucus, dissolves stagnation,
directs upwards, gets Qi moving und Yang.
Cooking time approx. 20 min
Calories p. portion: 47
3 portions

Quantity of ingredients:
Wakame 1 oz / 25g. (little) - cold - salty .... water
Water 2 cup / 450g. (yes) - cool - salty .... earth
Onion (shallot) 1-2 pcs. / 30g. (yes) - warm - acrid, sweet .... metal
Radish (white, green...) 1/8 lbs - 2oz / 50g. (yes) - cool - sweet, acrid ..... metal
Carrot 2 pieces / 180g. (yes) - neutral - sweet .... earth
Miso 2 table spoons / 20g. (yes) - neutral - salty .... water
Parsley 2 table spoons / 20g. (yes) - warm - bitter .... wood
Onion (spring onion) 1 table spoon (sliced) .... metal

Cooking instructions:
Soak wakame in water for a few minutes, remove and bring the water to
the boil. Add finely chopped onions and wakame, radishes and carrots,
cut into thin strips, and simmer for another 10 minutes. Dissolve miso in
a little cooled cooking water and add it at the end. Sprinkle with parsley
and spring onions.

9.25 Kuzu soup in the morning

Moisturizes, relaxes, builds up Qi, spreads, forces stomach, harmonizes
middle, reduces internal heat, detoxifies, softens, passes downwardly.
Cooking time approx. 5 min
Calories p. portion: 12
1 portion
Allergens: E

Quantity of ingredients:

Water 1 cup / 250g. (yes) - cool - salty................. ....earth
Soy sauce 1 dash / 2g. (little) - cold - salty............ ....water
Umeboshi paste 1 knife tip / 2g. (yes) - warm - sour..................................water

Cooking instructions:

Mix kuzu with cold water and heat till it boils while stirring. Once it is
glassy, remove from heat and let cool. Season
with Tamari and Umeboshipaste or crushed umeboshi plums
There is always the possibility to support your stomach and intestines
with this recipe, taken before the right breakfast.
A morning cure for stomach and mucous membranes. Fix the base
balance.

9.26 Lamb leg in the oven

Strengthens spleen and kidney Yang, relieves weakness, forces Qi,
heats middle and lower heater, forces Qi, forces spleen, relieves
inflammation, moisturizes, relaxes, builds up Qi, spreads, nourishes
liver-Yin, cools heat, produces humors.
Cooking time approx. 2 hours
Calories p. portion: 484
6 portions

Quantity of ingredients:

Lamb meat 2,2 lbs (leg) / 1000g. (little) - warm - sweet................................fire
Olive oil 2 table spoons / 20g. (rec.) - cool - sweet. ....earth
Potato 1,1 lbs / 500g. (yes) - neutral - sweet.......... ....earth
Onion (shallot) 3 pieces / 50g. (yes) - warm - acrid, sweet.......................metal
Pepper (ground) 1 pinch / 0,2g. () - warm - acrid ... .metal
Salt 1 pinch / 0,5g. (little) - cold - salty ....water
Tomato 4-5 pieces / 200g. (little) - cold - sweet-sour ....wood
Pepper powder (hot) 1 pinch / 0,5g. (yes) - warm - bitter..............................fire
Rosemary 1 pinch / 0,2g. (yes) - warm - bitter ....fire
Thyme 1 pinch / 0,2g. (rec.) - warm - bitter ....*
Savory 1 teaspoon / 1g. (yes) - warm - bitter ....water

Cooking instructions:

Put the leg of lamb on a baking tray painted with olive oil.
Distribute peeled and quartered potatoes and the quartered onions on
the plate.
Sprinkle with pepper, salt; add tomatoes roughly cut; dust with rose
paprika; drizzle with olive oil; sprinkle dried rosemary, savory, thyme
over it.
Bake at 250°C/482°F for 15 minutes; then reduce the heat to

150°C/302°F and bake for another 1 1/2 hours; occasionally drizzle some water over.
This fits: dry red wine, endive, radicchio, frisée or corn salad and millet.

9.27 Legumes

Strengthens spleen and liver, regulates Qi flow, moisturizes, relaxes, builds up Qi, spreads, nourishes blood and Qi, diuretic, harmonizes Qi (in the middle and lower heater), detoxifies, reduces internal heat and moisture.
Cooking time approx. 30 min
Calories p. portion: 31
5 portions

Quantity of ingredients:
Pinto beans speckled 1/4 lbs - 4oz / 100g. (yes) - neutral - sweet .... water
Lentils 1/8 lbs - 2oz / 50g. (yes) - neutral - sweet, sour .... water
Peas, green 1/8 lbs - 2oz / 50g. (yes) - neutral - sweet .... water
Water 4 cup / 1000g. (yes) - cool - salty .... earth
Lemon 1 slice / 2g. (omit) - cold - sour .... wood
Juniper berry 6 pieces / 2g. (rec.) - warm - sweet, acrid, bitter .... fire
Thyme 1 Twig / 3g. (rec.) - warm - bitter .... *
Rosemary 1 Twig / 3g. (yes) - warm - bitter .... fire
Carrot 1 piece / 100g. (yes) - neutral - sweet .... earth
Savory 1-2 teaspoons / 5g. (yes) - warm - bitter .... water
Ginger fresh a great piece / 3g. (rec.) - warm - acrid .... metal
Bay leaf 2-3 leaves / 1g. (yes) - warm - acrid .... metal
Wakame 1-2 strips / 1g. (little) - cold - salty .... water

Cooking instructions:
Legumes such as beans, lentils, peas or chickpeas are soaked in plenty of cold water for several hours to three days. The water should be changed every 8 hours. Then pour off soaking water and wash legumes thoroughly.

Preparation:
Cook the legumes with fresh cold water and a slice of ginger and bring to froth. Cook without lid for about 5 minutes, scooping off the foam. Only then add the following ingredients: a slice of lemon or lemon juice, crush juniper berries, thyme; (possibly 1 knife tip of asafoetida in case of severe indigestion). Add savory, sage, juniper, fenugreek seeds, carrots, bay leaves, fresh ginger, wakame algae.

Simmer on the slightest flame until beans or lentils have the desired consistency. This base can be stored for 3-4 days in the refrigerator.

9.28 Lentils and rice stew

Strengthens spleen and liver, regulates Qi flow, moisturizes, relaxes, builds up Qi, spreads, warms the stomach
and spleen, harmonizes the intestine, forces Qi, reduces moisture, brings the liver Qi in motion, cools heat.
Cooking time approx. 25 min
Calories p. portion: 232
3 portions
Allergens: LNO

Quantity of ingredients:
Lentils 1/4 lbs - 4oz / 100g. (yes) - neutral - sweet, sour .... water
Water 5 cups / 500g. (yes) - cool - salty .... earth
Rice variety any 1 cup / 120g. (little) - warm - sweet .... metal
Sesame oil 1 table spoon / 10g. (yes) - cool - sweet .... earth
Carrot 2 pieces / 150g. (yes) - neutral - sweet .... earth
Celery sticks 2 rods / 20g. (little) - cool - sweet .... earth
Cumin (Caraway seed) 1 pinch / 0,2g. (yes) - warm - acrid .... metal
Salt 1 pinch / 0,5g. (little) - cold - salty .... water
Vinegar (Apple vinegar) 1 dash / 2g. (little) - warm - sour, bitter .... wood
Parsley 2 table spoons / 18g. (yes) - warm - bitter .... wood

Cooking instructions:
Soak the dry lentils the day before.
Heat sesame oil in a hot pot; cut carrot and celery into small pieces and sauté; add rice, a pinch of cumin and lentils
and heat till it boils.
If the lenses are soft, add salt; season with a little vinegar and garnish with parsley.

Variant: In summer you can omit the cumin and add fresh green peas, Chinese cabbage or celery.

9.29 Millet with egg and butter

Forces blood, Yin and Jing, nourishes Yin, moisturizes in case of internal dryness, forces blood, forces spleen, calms nerves and stomach, strengthens spleen and kidney, diuretic, strengthens Qi and kidney Jing, moisturizes, relaxes, builds up Qi, spreads
Cooking time approx. 25 min
Calories p. portion: 338
2 portions
Allergens: CG

Quantity of ingredients:

Millet 1 cup / 100g. (yes) - cool - sweet, salty...earth
Ginger fresh 1/2 teaspoon / 1g. (rec.) - warm - acrid................................metal
Salt 1 pinch / 0,5g. (little) - cold - salty ....water
Parsley 2 table spoons / 16g. (yes) - warm - bitter....................................wood
Pepper powder (hot) 1 pinch / 1g. (yes) - warm - bitter................................fire
Chicken egg 2 pieces / 100g. (little) - neutral - sweet................................earth
Butter organic 2 table spoons / 20g. (little) - neutral - sweet ....earth
Nutmeg 1 pinch / 0,2g. (rec.) - warm - acrid..metal
Water 1 1/2 cups / 200g. (yes) - cool - salty...earth

Cooking instructions:

Simmer the millet with the ginger and nutmeg in the water for 5 min.
and let it swell for another 30 min.
Cook and peel 1 soft egg per person; pile up the millet on plates and
place 1 egg each in a hollow in the millet mountain; Put butter flakes
over it. Sprinkle with chopped parsley and the rose paprika.

9.30 Minestrone

Forces Qi of the middle, cools heat, diuretic, cools blood, reduces
mucus, reduces heat, moisturizes, relaxes, builds up Qi, spreads.
nourishes liver-Yin, cools heat, produces humors.
Cooking time approx. 30 min
Calories p. portion: 211
4 portions
Allergens: GL

Quantity of ingredients:

Onion (shallot) 2 pieces / 40g. (yes) - warm - acrid, sweet.......................metal
Sunflower oil 1 teaspoon / 10g. (little) - cool - sweet ....earth
Water 2 cup / 480g. (yes) - cool - salty...earth
Carrot 2 pieces / 120g. (yes) - neutral - sweet ....earth
Savoy cabbage / kale 1 handful / 15g. (yes) - neutral - sweet....................earth
Beans (green, fresh) 1 handful / 20g. (little) - neutral - sweet...................water
Celery sticks 3 pieces / 20g. (little) - cool - sweet......................................earth
Peas, green 4 table spoons / 30g. (yes) - neutral - sweet ....water
Zucchini 1 piece / 200g. (little) - cool - sweet ....earth
Rice variety any 1 cup / 120g. (little) - warm - sweet..................................metal
Bay leaf 3 leaves / 1g. (yes) - warm - acrid...metal
Sunflower oil 1 table spoon / 10g. (little) - cool - sweet ....earth
Salt 1 pinch / 1g. (little) - cold - salty ....water
Tomato 3 pieces / 150g. (little) - cold - sweet-sour....................................wood
Thyme 1 Twig / 3g. (rec.) - warm - bitter .... *
Basil 4 leaves / 2g. (rec.) - warm - acrid, bitter...fire

Cooking instructions:
Fry the onion in oil in a glassy saucepan and add water. Add vegetables, rice and salt and simmer gently. If the vegetables are firm, add tomatoes, a small sprig of thyme, basil and bay leaf and leave to simmer. Serve with Parmesan.

9.31 Polenta with ratatouille

Strengthens stomach Qi, diuretic, moisturizes relaxes, builds up Qi, spreads, nourishes liver-Yin, cools heat, produces humors, cools and moves blood, reduces external and internal wind, reduces internal heat.
Cooking time approx. 30 min
Calories p. portion: 226
4 portions
Allergens: G

Quantity of ingredients:
Corn Grease (Polenta) 1 cup / 120g. (little) - neutral - sweet ....earth
Water 1 1/2 cups / 240g. (yes) - cool - salty..earth
Aubergine 1 piece (large) / 200g. (little) - cool - sweet ....earth
Zucchini 2 pieces / 500g. (little) - cool - sweet ....earth
Onion white 2 pieces / 120g. (yes) - warm - acrid .... metal
Tomato 2 pieces (blended) / 200g. (little) - cold - sweet-sour.................... wood
Olive oil 2 table spoons / 20g. (rec.) - cool - sweet.....................................earth
Salt 1 pinch / 0,5g. (little) - cold - salty .... water
Parsley 1 table spoon (chopped) / 8g. (yes) - warm - bitter....................... wood
Thyme 1/2 teaspoon / 1g. (rec.) - warm - bitter .... *
Spring onion 2 table spoons (chopped) / 12g. (yes) - warm - acrid .... metal
Basil 4 leaves / 2g. (rec.) - warm - acrid, bitter...fire

Cooking instructions:
Use double the amount of water to polenta, add salt and oil and heat till it boils. Stir in polenta, stirring constantly. Take off the fire and let it swell for 20 minutes. Meanwhile, cut the onion, fry in a saucepan with hot oil. Add the diced zucchini, tomatoes and melanzani and simmer for about 20 minutes. Add basil, thyme, salt.
Coat baking tray with oil, apply polenta evenly and wait until it gets stronger.
Add the cooked ratatouille to polenta, portion and then put in the oven for a few minutes (possibly with grated parmesan).
Sprinkle with fresh parsley and finely chopped spring onion.
The valuable tip: The Polenta sections are ideal for on the go.

9.32 Potatoes with wild garlic-curd cheese

Forces Qi, forces spleen, relieves inflammation, nourishes blood and Yi, forces Zang-organs, forces stomach and intestines, harmonizes Qi, relieves alcohol poisoning, moisturizes lungs, gets Qi moving.
Cooking time approx. 20 min
Calories p. portion: 254
2 portions
Allergens: G

Quantity of ingredients:
Potato 3/4 lbs / 300g. (yes) - neutral - sweet..earth
Salt 1 pinch / 0,1g. (little) - cold - salty ....water
Wild garlic 2 handful / 30g. (yes) - warm - sweet, little acrid......................metal
Curd cheese 20% 5/8 lbs - 8oz / 250g. (yes) - cool - sour.........................wood
Yogurt (natural, 1.5% fat) 2 table spoons / 20g. (rec.) - cool - sour...........wood
Salt 1 pinch / 1g. (little) - cold - salty ....water

Cooking instructions:
Cook potatoes in salted water and peel.
Wash he wild garlic leaves and carefully dried and cut into fine strips.
Mix the cottage cheese, yogurt and salt and mix in the chopped wild garlic pieces. Serve with the potatoes.
In the season in which no wild garlic grows the wild garlic pesto can be used.

9.33 Pumpkin curry

Forces lungs and spleen, diuretic, forces Qi, protects liver, warms the stomach and spleen, harmonizes the intestine, forces Qi, reduces moisture, moisturizes, relaxes, builds up Qi, spreads, nourishes blood and liver, harmonizes liver and spleen.
Cooking time approx. 20 min
Calories p. portion: 193
3 portions

Quantity of ingredients:
Pumpkin 3/4 lbs / 300g. (yes) - warm - sweet ....earth
Olive oil 2 table spoons / 30g. (rec.) - cool - sweet.....................................earth
Coriander 1 pinch / 1g. (yes) - warm - acrid ....metal
Pepper (ground) 1 pinch / 0,5g. () - warm - acrid ....metal
Curry 1 pinch / 1g. (yes) - warm - acrid ....metal
Water 1/4 cup / 50g. (yes) - cool - salty...earth
Salt 1 pinch / 1g. (little) - cold - salty ....water
Parsley 1 table spoon / 7g. (yes) - warm - bitter..wood

Cardamom 1 pinch / 1g. (little) - warm - acrid .... metal
Turmeric (yellow root) 1 pinch / 1g. (yes) - warm - bitter .... *
Rice (whole grain) 1/2 cup / 60g. (rec.) - warm - sweet .... metal
Water 3 cups / 300g. (yes) - cool - salty .... earth
Salt 1 pinch / 1g. (little) - cold - salty .... water

Cooking instructions:

Heat olive oil in pan. Steam the pumpkin cut in cubes, season with cilantro, pepper and curry, simmer with a little water, salt with sea salt, add chopped parsley with cardamom and turmeric, simmer on a small fire for about 10 minutes, depending on the pumpkin, the pumpkin should still be firm.

Place the rice in salted water, bring to the boil and let it simmer over low heat for about 15 minutes.

9.34 Pumpkin soup

Forces lungs and spleen, diuretic, forces Qi, protects liver, forces Qi, forces spleen, relieves inflammation, moisturizes, relaxes, builds up Qi, spreads, strengthens spleen and liver, regulates Qi flow, moisturizes, relaxes, builds up Qi, spreads.
Cooking time approx. 1 hour
Calories p. portion: 105
3 portions

Quantity of ingredients:

Pumpkin 3/4 lbs / 300g. (yes) - warm - sweet .... earth
Carrot 2 pieces / 100g. (yes) - neutral - sweet .... earth
Potato 2 pieces / 120g. (yes) - neutral - sweet .... earth
Olive oil 1 table spoon / 10g. (rec.) - cool - sweet .... earth
Onion white 1 piece / 50g. (yes) - warm - acrid .... metal
Water 1 cup / 120g. (yes) - cool - salty .... earth
Parsley 1 table spoon / 7g. (yes) - warm - bitter .... wood
Anise (Common Fennel) 1 pinch / 1g. (yes) - warm - acrid .... earth
Salt 1 pinch / 1g. (little) - cold - salty .... water

Cooking instructions:

Add the olive oil to the pan, add the diced pumpkin, diced carrots and potatoes. Roast them shortly, add the finely chopped onion, fill with water, add enough water to cover the vegetables at least 3 finger-widths. Boil at low heat.
Season with sea salt, add small cutted parsley, a pinch of anise (little). Allow to simmer for about 35 minutes. Then purée the soup and add some water, depending on the consistency of the soup.

9.35 Pumpkin-yoghurt soup

Moisturizes, relaxes, builds up Qi, spreads, strengthens spleen and liver, regulates Qi flow, moisturizes dryness, preserves the fluids, contracts, gets Qi moving, forces fluid production, reduces cold-evil, directs upwards.
Cooking time approx. 15 min
Calories p. portion: 68
4 portions
Allergens: GL

Quantity of ingredients:
Basic recipe for a vegetable soup (nutritious) 1 cup / 300g. (rec.) - neutral - *. *
Hokkaido pumpkin 1,1 lbs / 500g. (little) - warm - sweet ....earth
Ginger fresh 1/2 teaspoon / 2g. (rec.) - warm - acrid.................................metal
Anise (Common Fennel) 1/4 teaspoon / 1g. (yes) - warm - acrid ....earth
Yogurt (natural, 1.5% fat) 3/8 lbs - 6oz / 150g. (rec.) - cool - sour............. wood
Peppermint 2 leaves / 1g. (little) - cool - acrid, bitter ....metal
Salt 1 pinch / 1g. (little) - cold - salty ....water

Cooking instructions:
Heat the vegetable broth (after the basic recipe) till it boils. Add diced pumpkin, chopped ginger, crushed fennel seeds and anise. Bring the soup to the boil and simmer for about 12 minutes until the pumpkin is soft.
Remove soup from the heat. Puree the soup with the yoghurt with the blender. Serve soup with finely chopped mint sprinkled.

9.36 Quinoa piquant with avocado

Nourishes Yin from liver, lungs and colon, moisturizes, relaxes, builds up Qi, spreads, strengthens spleen and liver, regulates Qi flow, moisturizes, relaxes, builds up Qi, spreads, forces Qi, dries out, regulates Qi, warms spleen and kidney, dissolves st
Cooking time approx. 20 min
Calories p. portion: 561
2 portions

Quantity of ingredients:
Water 1 1/2 cups / 240g. (yes) - cool - salty ....earth
Quinoa 1 cup / 100g. (rec.) - neutral - sweet, sour ....fire
Carrot 1 piece shredded / 100g. (yes) - neutral - sweet ....earth
Spring onion 2 table spoons (chopped) / 12g. (yes) - warm - acrid .... metal
Turmeric (yellow root) 1/2 teaspoon / 1g. (yes) - warm - bitter......................... *
Avocado 1 piece soft / 300g. (little) - cold - sweet ....earth

Salt 1 pinch / 0,5g. (little) - cold - salty .... water
Pepper (ground) 1 pinch / 0,2g. () - warm - acrid .... metal
Linseed oil 2 teaspoons / 4g. (rec.) - neutral - sweet.................................earth

Cooking instructions:
Put quinoa in hot water.
Add grated carrot, pepper and salt, finely chopped spring onion and turmeric.
Simmer about 20 minutes, pull from the fire.
Add pre-cut avocado.
Add a dash of oil and sprinkle with fresh parsley and gomasio.
Spices and herbs: turmeric, cardamom, cress. parsley, chives.
Variation: For those who want more hearty, you can also use a sardine from organic fish preserves. If you are the "protein type", this breakfast will hold on for a long time!

9.37 Reissue soup with duck

Nourishes Yin, warms the stomach and spleen, harmonizes the intestine, forces Qi, reduces moisture, nourishes blood and liver, harmonizes liver and spleen, moisturizes, relaxes, builds up Qi, spreads.
Cooking time approx. 1 1/2 hours
Calories p. portion: 161
6 portions
Allergens: EG

Quantity of ingredients:
Rice round grain 1 cup / 100g. (little) - neutral - sweet............................. metal
Water 8 cups / 900g. (yes) - cool - salty..earth
Duck (slaughtered) 5/8 lbs - 8oz / 250g. (yes) - cool - sweet, salty .... wood
Shiitake, dried 4-6 pieces / 5g. (little) - neutral - sweet...............................earth
Parsley 2 table spoons / 12g. (yes) - warm - bitter .... wood
Butter organic 1 teaspoon / 3g. (little) - neutral - sweet..............................earth
Soy sauce 1 dash / 2g. (little) - cold - salty... water

Cooking instructions:
Soak shiitake mushrooms. Prepare rice soup according to the basic recipe. Add duck meat and shiitake mushrooms
for the last 30 minutes. Add oyster mushrooms, parsley and a little butter at the very end. Season with soy sauce.

Variant: Add soaked and cooked adzuki beans. They enhance the diuretic effect.

9.38 Reissue soup with seaweed

Forces Qi and blood, reduces cold, forces spleen, liver and stomach, strengthens blood and Qi, regulates Qi, warms spleen and kidney, dissolves stagnation, directs upwards.
Cooking time approx. 4-5 hours
Calories p. portion: 130
6 portions
Allergens: L

Quantity of ingredients:
Beef meatbones 3/4 lbs / 10g. (little) - warm - sweet ....earth
Beef soup meat 7/8 lbs / 400g. (little) - warm - sweet ....earth
Parsley 1/4 Bunch / 25g. (yes) - warm - bitter ....wood
Juniper berry 4 pieces / 2g. (rec.) - warm - sweet, acrid, bitter......................fire
Carrot 2 pieces / 180g. (yes) - neutral - sweet ....earth
Celery root 1/4 lbs / 100g. (little) - cool - sweet ....earth
Onion (spring onion) 1/2 piece / 10g. (yes) - warm - acrid........................metal
Peppercorns 4 pieces / 1g. (little) - warm - acrid ....metal
Lovage 1 Twig / 3g. (yes) - warm - acrid, bitter ....metal
Wakame 1 inch / 3g. (little) - cold - salty..water
Rice variety any 3 table spoons / 20g. (little) - warm - sweet ....metal
Water 4 cup / 900g. (yes) - cool - salty..earth

Cooking instructions:
Boil parsley in water. Add the juniper berries, meat bones, a piece of soup, carrot and a piece of celery tuber, a separately tanned onion half, a few peppery grains, a belly and a piece of wakame algae; Allow 4-8 hours to simmer and then strain. Add the rice and simmer for another 1/2 hour.

Keep the stock in the refrigerator.

Variant: If you remove the meat after 1-2 hours, you can still dice it well and use it later as a supporter.

9.39 Rice congee with carrots and fennel

Nutritious builds up Qi, forces the digestive functions.
Cooking time approx. 2 hours and more
Calories p. portion: 131
3 portions
Allergens: G

Quantity of ingredients:

Basic recipe for a rice soup (Congee) 2 cup / 500g. (yes) - neutral - sweet ..... *
Carrot 2 pieces / 100g. (yes) - neutral - sweet ....earth
Fennel 1 piece / 250g. (little) - warm - sweet, little acrid.............................earth
Butter organic 1 teaspoon / 3g. (little) - neutral - sweet..............................earth
Cardamom 1/2 teaspoon / 1g. (little) - warm - acrid .... metal

Cooking instructions:

Cook rice congee according to basic recipe.
Clean and cut carrots and fennel.

When carrots and fennel are cooked from the beginning, they serve
wholesomeness. If added shortly before the end of the cooking time,
taste and vitamins are retained.

Refine with butter and cardamom before serving.

9.40 Rice dulse soup

Strengthens spleen and liver, regulates Qi flow, relaxes, builds up Qi,
spreads, dries out, passes downwardly, strengthens stomach Qi, warms
the stomach and spleen, harmonizes the intestine, forces Qi, reduces
moisture.
Cooking time approx. 5 min
Calories p. portion: 190
2 portions
Allergens: L

Quantity of ingredients:

Basic recipe for a rice soup (Congee) 4 cups / 500g. (yes) - neutral - sweet ... *
Basic recipe for a vegetable soup (nutritious) 2 cup / 500g. (rec.) - neutral - *. *
Dulse (seaweed) 2 table spoons / 15g. (yes) - neutral - salty...................water

Cooking instructions:

Worm up a portion of pre-cooked basic recipe for a ricesoup (congee)
and a portion pre-cooked basic recipe for a vegetable soup.
Bake the dulse in the oven at 220 degrees for 3 minutes. Spread the
crisp dulse over the rice.

9.41 Rice noodle soup with shiitake mushrooms

Strengthens spleen and liver, regulates Qi flow, relaxes, builds up Qi, spreads, dries out, passes downwardly, strengthens stomach Qi, nourishes Yin of the lungs, stomach and colon, supports digestion, reduces internal wind.
Cooking time approx. 20 min
Calories p. portion: 66
2 portions
Allergens: L

Quantity of ingredients:

Rice noodles 2 handful / 20g. (little) - neutral - sweet .... metal
Shiitake, dried 4-6 pieces / 5g. (little) - neutral - sweet............................... earth
Basic recipe for a vegetable soup 1 1/2 cups / 240g. (rec.) - neutral - *........... *
Chinese cabbage 1 cup / 60g. (little) - cool - sweet................................... earth
Lovage 1 teaspoon / 3g. (yes) - warm - acrid, bitter .... metal
Miso 2 table spoons / 18g. (yes) - neutral - salty...................................... water

Cooking instructions:

Soak rice noodles and shiitake mushrooms separately in cold water. Heat the vegetable broth and add the soaked shiitake mushrooms cut into strips and simmer gently. Cut Chinese cabbage into noodles, add lovage green and rice noodles and let it steep for a while. Before serving, stir in Miso dissolved in a little cooled water.
Recommendation: Suitable at the beginning of each meal, also for breakfast

9.42 Rice soup with grated carrots and fresh herbs

Strengthens spleen and liver, regulates Qi flow, moisturizes, relaxes, builds up Qi, spreads, forces kidney and bladder.
Cooking time approx. 5 min
Calories p. portion: 131
4 portions
Allergens: EG

Quantity of ingredients:

Rice wild (nature rice) 1 cup / 100g. (rec.) - neutral - sweet, bitter .... metal
Water 6 cups / 700g. (yes) - cool - salty .... earth
Carrot 1 piece / 100g. (yes) - neutral - sweet .... earth
Soy sauce 1 dash / 2g. (little) - cold - salty .... water
Butter organic 1 teaspoon / 3g. (little) - neutral - sweet............................. earth
Ground 1 pinch / 0,3g. (little) - warm - acrid .... metal
Turmeric (yellow root) 1 pinch / 0,2g. (yes) - warm - bitter .... *

Cooking instructions:

In a portion of rice congee according to basic recipe, softly cook a grated carrot, add butter and soy sauce.
Sprinkle with fresh herbs.
Spices and herbs: black cumin, turmeric, cardamom, parsley, sage, thyme, basil, rosemary.
Winter: parsnip, celery, onion, leek, pumpkin
Summer: tomatoes, zucchini, spring onion, radishes, arugula.

9.43 Sliced chicken with walnuts and sherry

Warming and nourishing, directs the Qi upwards, forces blood, spleen and kidney.
Cooking time approx. 25 min
Calories p. portion: 304
4 portions
Allergens: EGHN

Quantity of ingredients:

Butter organic 2 table spoons / 35g. (little) - neutral - sweet .... earth
Walnuts 2 table spoons / 25g. (little) - warm - sweet .... earth
Ginger fresh 1/2 teaspoon / 2g. (rec.) - warm - acrid .... metal
Onion (shallot) 2 pieces / 40g. (yes) - warm - acrid, sweet .... metal
Salt 1 pinch / 1g. (little) - cold - salty .... water
Chicken meat 3/4 lbs / 300g. (rec.) - warm - sweet .... wood
Sesame, white 1 teaspoon / 2g. (yes) - neutral - sweet .... earth
Black fungus mushroom 4 pieces / 3g. (yes) - neutral - sweet .... earth
Shiitake, dried 4 pieces / 5g. (little) - neutral - sweet .... earth
Soy sauce 1 dash / 3g. (little) - cold - salty. .... water
Rice (whole grain) 1 cup / 120g. (rec.) - warm - sweet .... metal
Water 6 cups / 550g. (yes) - cool - salty .... earth
Salt 1 pinch / 1g. (little) - cold - salty .... water

Cooking instructions:

Heat butter or sesame oil in a hot pan; Sauté walnuts, copious grated ginger, chopped shallots or onions; Add the salt and the sliced chicken and sauté everything; Rose paprika, roasted sesame, soaked black fungus, shiitake mushrooms or mushrooms; with a shot sherry; infuse with water; Simmer for 5 to 10 minutes until the meat is cooked; Season with soy sauce.
Place the rice in salted water, heat till it boils and let it simmer over low heat for about 15 minutes.
This fits: lamb's lettuce, Radicchio

9.44 Soup with egg yolk

Forces Qi and Yang, is very warming.
Cooking time approx. 5 min
Calories p. portion: 173
1 portion
Allergens: CO

Quantity of ingredients:
Basic recipe for a beef soup (warming) 5/8 lbs - 8oz / 250g. (yes) - warm - * .. *
Chicken yolk 1 piece / 25g. (yes) - neutral - sweet.....................................earth

Cooking instructions:
Warm the beef soup according to the basic recipe for a beef broth,
warm it up and jell the yolk.

9.45 Sweet potato pancakes with basil pesto

Forces Qi, blood, Yin and Jing.
Cooking time approx. 30 min
Calories p. portion: 625
3 portions
Allergens: ACH

Quantity of ingredients:
Sweet potato 4 pieces / 500g. (yes) - warm - sweet...................................earth
Onion read 1/2 piece / 30g. (yes) - warm - acrid ....metal
Basil 1 table spoon / 10g. (rec.) - warm - acrid, bitter....................................fire
Chicken egg 2 pieces / 140g. (little) - neutral - sweet...............................earth
Spelled wholemeal flour 3 oz / 80g. (yes) - neutral - sweet.......................wood
Salt 1 pinch / 0,5g. (little) - cold - salty ....water
Olive oil 1/4 cup / 20g. (rec.) - cool - sweet ....earth
Salt 1 teaspoon (coarse) / 3g. (little) - cold - salty ....water
Basil 1 handful / 15g. (rec.) - warm - acrid, bitter...fire
Parsley 1 handful / 15g. (yes) - warm - bitter..wood
Garlic 2 cloves / 3g. (rec.) - hot - acrid ....metal
Walnuts 1/8 lbs - 2oz / 60g. (little) - warm - sweet...................................earth
Olive oil 2 table spoons / 20g. (rec.) - cool - sweet...................................earth

Cooking instructions:
Sweet Potato Buffer: Wash the sweet potato thoroughly, but do not
peel, and grate into a large bowl. Add onion, basil, egg and flour, mix
well and sprinkle with salt. The mixture can be formed into buffers. Bake
in a preheated tube on a baking tray coated with oil for 4 to 5 minutes
on both sides.

Basil Pesto: Add the salt, chopped basil and parsley and crushed garlic in a small bowl and crush (if available, use the mortar). Add the grated walnuts. While stirring, add enough olive oil until the desired consistency is achieved.

9.46 Tea from bearberry leaf

Cools damp heat in the bladder.
Cooking time approx. 10 min
Calories p. portion: 0
4 portions

Quantity of ingredients:
Bearberry leaf 2 table spoons / 8g. (yes) - cool - bitter..................................... *
Water 2 cup / 500g. (yes) - cool - salty..earth

Cooking instructions:
Heat the water till it boils and put it aside. Add grape leaves and leave for 10 min. to let go. Sweet to taste with honey. Strain when pouring.

9.47 Tea from cinnamon sticks

Warms the stomach and spleen, promotes blood circulation and conduction flow, relieves cold-sickness and pain.
Cooking time approx. 15 min
Calories p. portion: 2
1 portion

Quantity of ingredients:
Cinnamon sticks 1/4 piece / 1g. (rec.) - hot - acrid, sweet................................ *
Water 1 cup / 125g. (yes) - cool - salty..earth

Cooking instructions:
A quarter of a cinnamon stick for a cup of tea. Start cold and bring to the boil. Let it sit for 15 minutes, then strain.
This tea is unsweetened and swallowed, slowly drunk. The amount is enough for one day.

9.48 Tea from juniper berry

Dries out, passes downwardly, activates Wei Qi.
Cooking time approx. 10 min
Calories p. portion: 10
1 portion

Quantity of ingredients:
Juniper berry 1 teaspoon / 3g. (rec.) - warm - sweet, acrid, bitter ....fire
Water 1 cup / 125g. (yes) - cool - salty...earth

Cooking instructions:
A teaspoon of dried juniper berries for a cup of tea. Start cold and bring to the boil. Let it sit for 15 minutes, then strain.
This tea is unsweetened and swallowed, slowly drunk. The amount is enough for one day.

9.49 Tea from rosemary

Dries out, passes downwardly, forces heart, lung and spleen Qi, forces liver-blood, forces heart-Yin, expels spleen heat / cold moisture, strengthens spleen and kidney Yang.
Cooking time approx. 15 min
Calories p. portion: 1
4 portions

Quantity of ingredients:
Rosemary 2-4 teaspoons / 6g. (yes) - warm - bitter ....fire
Water 2 cup / 500g. (yes) - cool - salty...earth

Cooking instructions:
Heat the water till it boils and put it aside. Add rosemary and 10 min. to let go. Strain. Sweet to taste with honey.

9.50 Tea from thyme

Converts mucus, forces lungs and spleen, dries out, passes downwardly.
Cooking time approx. 10 min
Calories p. portion: 0
4 portions

Quantity of ingredients:
Thyme 3 table spoons / 6g. (rec.) - warm - bitter.. *
Water 2 cup water / 500g. (yes) - cool - salty...earth

Cooking instructions:
Heat the water till it boils and put it aside. Add thyme and 10 min. to let go. Strain. Sweet to taste with honey.
Drink 2 to 3 cups daily by mouth

9.51 Thick pea soup

Nourishes Qi, diuretic, harmonizes Qi (especially in the Middle and Lower), strengthens the kidney and the defense Qi, dischars moisture.
Cooking time approx. 2-3 hours
Calories p. portion: 123
3 portions
Allergens: AN

Quantity of ingredients:
Peas, green 3/8 lbs - 6oz / 150g. (yes) - neutral - sweet............................ water
Water 2 1/4 cups / 550g. (yes) - cool - salty..earth
Sesame oil 1 table spoon / 20g. (yes) - cool - sweet...................................earth
Onion white 1/2 piece / 25g. (yes) - warm - acrid.. metal
Ginger fresh 1/2 teaspoon / 1g. (rec.) - warm - acrid................................. metal
Ground 1/2 teaspoon / 1g. (little) - warm - acrid.. metal
Oat meal 1 table spoon / 15g. (little) - warm - sweet................................. metal
Salt 1 pinch / 1g. (little) - cold - salty .... water
Parsley 1 stem / 2g. (yes) - warm - bitter... wood

Cooking instructions:
Soak dried peas before cooking. Sauté sesame oil, onion, a little oatmeal, ginger and cumin in a hot pot; add the peas and simmer for 2-3 hours; add salt at the end and purée with a blender; garnish with parsley.

9.52 Vegetable semolina soup

Strengthens spleen and liver, regulates Qi flow, builds up Qi, dries out, passes downwardly, reduces moisture, regulates Qi.
Cooking time approx. 20 min
Calories p. portion: 199
3 portions
Allergens: AEGL

Quantity of ingredients:
Basic recipe for a vegetable soup (nutritious) 2 cup / 500g. (rec.) - neutral - *. *
Potato 1 piece / 80g. (yes) - neutral - sweet...earth
Parsnip 1 piece / 180g. (rec.) - cool - bitter ....fire
Carrot 1 piece / 120g. (yes) - neutral - sweet ....earth
Celery root 3/8 lbs - 6oz / 150g. (little) - cool - sweet ....earth
Kohlrabi 1/2 piece / 200g. (yes) - neutral - acrid, sweet ....earth
Beans (green, fresh) 1/4 lbs / 100g. (little) - neutral - sweet...................... water

Wheat semolina 2 table spoons / 24g. (omit) - cool - sweet, salty............. wood
Lovage 1/2 teaspoon / 2g. (yes) - warm - acrid, bitter............................... metal
Butter organic 1 table spoon / 20g. (little) - neutral - sweet........................earth
Soy sauce 1 teaspoon / 3g. (little) - cold - salty... water

Cooking instructions:
Worm the prepared vegetable soup; cook the vegetables in the soup softly. Spread some wheatgrass and let it swell. At the end, add lovage-green and a little butter and taste with soy sauce.

9.53 Yellow lentil soup

Reduces internal heat and moisture, softens, passes downwardly, moves Qi and blood, diuretic, reduces moisture, strengthens spleen and liver, regulates Qi flow, builds up Qi.
Cooking time approx. 20 min
Calories p. portion: 155
7 portions
Allergens: A

Quantity of ingredients:
Lentils yellow 1 lbs / 500g. (yes) - neutral - sweet, sour........................... water
Carrot 2 pieces / 150g. (yes) - neutral - sweet ....earth
Kohlrabi 1 piece / 300g. (yes) - neutral - acrid, sweet ....earth
Onion white 1 piece / 50g. (yes) - warm - acrid.. metal
Parsley 1/2 bunch / 100g. (yes) - warm - bitter... wood
Turmeric (yellow root) 1 pinch / 1g. (yes) - warm - bitter .... *
Cardamom 1 pinch / 1g. (little) - warm - acrid .... metal
Salt 1 pinch / 1g. (little) - cold - salty .... water
Olive oil 1 table spoon / 10g. (rec.) - cool - sweet ....earth
Water 4 cup / 1000g. (yes) - cool - salty..earth
Lemon juice 1/2 piece / 15g. (omit) - cold - sour .... wood
White bread (wheat bread) 7 slices / 140g. (omit) - cool - sweet.............. wood

Cooking instructions:
Wash lenses well in a colander. Heat oil in a pot. Add finely chopped onion, sliced carrots, diced kohlrabi and spices, sauté and salt. Add the lentils and cover with water and simmer for 20 minutes. Add water as needed and season with salt. Sprinkle with fresh parsley or fresh green cilantro and drizzle with lemon juice.
Here you can also use red lenses. (same cooking time).
Serve with white bread.

10 Effects of food

10.1 Use ingredients: recommendable

Angelica root
Artichoke
Banana (cooking banana)
Basic recipe for a chicken soup (warming)
Basic recipe for a vegetable soup (nutritious)
Basil
Basil (fresh)
Blackthorn (Sloe)
Blue mallow tee
Boxhorn clover seeds
Broad beans (thick beans)
Buckwheat
Buckwheat (roasted) Kasha
Buttermilk
Chamomile
Chicken liver
Chicken meat
Chicory
Chinese pearl barley
Chocolate (Diabetic)
Cinnamon ground
Cinnamon sticks
Coffee
Cottage cheese
Cranberries
Cranberry jam
Curcuma
Daisy
Deer meat
Elderberries
Elderberry blossom tee
Fennel tea
Feta cheese
Garlic
Gelee Royal

Ginger fresh
Herring
Hibiscus tea
Juniper berry
Lemon Balm (dried)
Lemon Balm (fresh)
Linseed oil
Millet flakes
Nettles
Nutmeg
Olive oil
Parsnip
Poppy
Quail
Quinoa
Radicchio
Rapeseed oil
Rice (whole grain)
Rice w ld (nature rice)
Rose hip tea
Rye
Rye flour
Rye wholemeal bread
Slug
Sour milk
Stevia (candyleaf, sweetleaf)
Tea mixture uric acid lowering
Thyme
Tsampa (roasted barley flour)
Valerian
Walnut oil
Wheat germ oil
White beans
Yam root, yam root tuber
Yogurt (natural, 1.5% fat)
Yogurt (natural, 3.5% fat)

10.2 Use ingredients: yes

Acai powder
Adzuki beans
Agar agar (kelp)
Agrimony
Aloe juice
Amaranth Pops
Anise (Common Fennel)
Apple (sour)
Arrowroot

Asparagus (green or white)
Baking powder
Bamboo shoots
Banana
Banchatee (green tea)
barberry
Barley
Barley flour
Barley not peeled

Basic recipe for a beef soup
Basic recipe for a beef soup (warming)
Basic recipe for a duck soup
Basic recipe for a fish soup
Basic recipe for a rice soup (Congee)
Batavia
Bay leaf
Bearberry leaf
Beef heart (calf)
Beef stomach
Beer (alcohol-free)
Black beans
Black caraway
Black fungus mushroom
Black tea
Blackberry dried (unripe fruit)
Blackberry leaves
Black-eyed peas
Blueberry
Bocksdorn fruits (Fructus Lycii, Goji,
goji berry dried
Boletus mushroom
Borage
Borage oil
Brazil nuts
Bread with carob kernel flour
Brussels sprouts
Buckwheat whole grain
Bulgur (cereals)
Burdock root tea
Bush beans
Butter beans white
Camembert
Cantaloupe
Capers in olive oil
Carob flour, St. john's bread
Carrot
Carrot (Early Carrot)
Carrot juice without sugar
Caviar
Cereal coffee
Chamomile tea
Channa-Dal
Cherry (sour)
Chervil
Chicken heart
Chicken stomach
Chicken yolk
Chickpeas
Chickweed
Chili (pod or ground)
Chives
Chlorella (fresh water)
Chocolate

Clementine
Clove
Cocoa
Coconut flakes
Cod
Codfish
Coriander
Coriander (fresh)
Corn silk tea
Couscous
Cow's milk (1.5% fat)
Cow's milk (whole milk 3.5% fat)
Cream 10% coffee cream
Cream sour 10%
Cucumber
Cucumber (bitter)
Cucumber (spicy cucumber)
Cumin (Caraway seed)
Curd cheese 20%
Curry
Dandelion juice
Dandelionroots tea
Dashi
Deer meat
Deer's Bones
Dill
Duck (heart)
Duck (slaughtered)
Dulse (seaweed)
Dyer's broom herb
Edam cheese
Endive salad
Fennel seeds ground
Fenugreek (Trigonella foenum-
graecum)
Feta cheese
Fish innards
Fish pieces mixed (fresh water)
Fish remains
Flounder
Flower pollen
Fresh cheese
Fresh cheese from soya
Freshwater fish
Galangal
Garam Masala powder
Ginger oil
Ginger powder
Ginkgo fruit
Ginseng
Ginseng root
Goat
Goat and sheep's brain
Goat and sheep's liver

Goat and sheep's milk
Goat and sheep's stomach
Goat cheese
Goose
Goose parts
Grapeseed oil
Green spelt
Guava
Hawthorn
Hazelnuts
Herbs bitter
Herbs of Provence
Herbs various
Herbs wild
Hijiki
Hop
Horehound leaves
Hyssop
Iceberg lettuce
Jasmine blossoms tee
Jellyfish
Kalmus
Kefir
Kidney beans (red)
King Solomon's-seal
Kohlrabi
Kukicha tea
Kumquats
Lamb's lettuce
Lavender blossoms
Leaf salads (bitter)
Leek
Lemon peel
Lemongrass
Lentils
Lentils black
Lentils red
Lentils yellow
Licorice root tea
Lima beans
Lime blossom tea
Linseed
Linseed (crushed)
Liver smoothing tea
Longane
Loquate / Japanese medlar
Lotus seeds
Lovage
Lovage seeds
Mallow (Malva sylvestris) blossom tea
Manioc flour
Marjoram
Mediterranean fish (cod, plaice,
haddock, sea eel, mackerel)

Medlar
Millet
Minera water
Miso
Miso black (fermented)
Morel, dried
Mozzarella
Mu Erh Mushroom
Mullet
Mung bean sprouting
Mussels
Mustard
Mustard Dijon
Mustard medium hot
Mustard seeds
Mustard sweet
Noodles (whole grain) with egg
Oat
Oat flakes (whole grain)
Oat flour
Octopus
Octopus
Okra
Olives green
Onion (shallot)
Onion (spring onion)
Onion read
Onion white
Orange blossom
Orange grated peel
Oregaro dried
Oregaro fresh
Oyster shell powder
Oysters
Parsley
Parsley root
Passion blossoms tea
Pearl barley
Peas
Peas, green
Pepper powder (hot)
Peppers powder
Perch
Pheasant
Pig blood
Pigeon
Pigeon egg
Pimento
Pine nuts
Pinto beans speckled
Pistachios
Plaice
Pork brain
Pork lung

Pork stomach
Pork's intestine
Potato
Potato (mealy)
Potato flour
Prickly pear
Processed cheese 12%
Psyllium seed
Pumpkin
Quail egg
Rabbit meat
Radish (white, green, purple-red)
Radish black
Radish horseradish
Radish leaves
Raspberry
Raspberry dried (immature)
Raspberry leaf tea
Red beet
Red cabbage
Ribworttea
Rice black
Rice mash
Rice red
Romaine lettuce / lettuce salad
Rose blossom tea
Rose leaf tea
Rosefish
Rosemary
Safflower (Dyer's thistle / Hong Hua)
Saffron
Sago (cereals)
Salt (herbal)
Savory
Savoy cabbage / kale
Sea buckthorn
Sea cucumber
Seacrab
Sesame oil
Sesame oil roasted
Sesame paste (Tahini)
Sesame, black
Sesame, white
Sheep's milk
Sheep's milk yoghurt
Sorrel

Sour cream 15% fat
Soya Cuisine (soy cream)
Soybean milk
Soybean oil
Soybeans, black
Soybeans, yellow
Spelled (Dark) bread
Spelled flakes
Spelled grain
Spelled semolina
Spelled wholemeal flour
Spinach
Spiny lobsters
Spurdog (spiny dogfish, Schillerlocken)
St. Benedict's thistle, blessed thistle,
holy thistle, spotted thistle
Star anise
Sunflower seeds
Supplementary nutrition
Sweet potato
Thistle oil
Thyme dried
Trout
Truffle
Turkey breast meat
Turmeric (yellow root)
Turnip
Turnips
Umeboshi paste
Umeboshi plums (Japanese apricots)
Water
Water hot
Wheatgrass juice
Wheatgrass powder
Whey
White cabbage
Whitefish
Wild boar meat
Wild garlic (garlic spinach)
Wild herbs
Wormwood herb
Yarrow
Yarrow tea
Yeast
Yew nut
Yogi tea

10.3 Use ingredients: little

Agave nectar
Almond milk
Amaranth
Anchovy / Sardine

Apricot
Aubergine
Avocado
Barley grass powder

Barley grouts
Bean oil
Beans (green, fresh)
Beef fillet
Beef heart
Beef liver
Beef lungs (calf)
Beef meat
Beef meat (calf)
Beef meatbones
Beef Oxtail pieces
Beef soup meat
Berries of the season
Bitter liqueur
Blackberry´s
Blueberry juice
Bread roll
Breadcrumbs (wheat bread, bread roll)
Brie cheese
Broccoli
Buckbean
Butter (half fat)
Butter organic
Calamari
Carambola (Star fruit)
Cardamom
Carp
Cauliflower
Celery root
Celery sticks
Chanterelle
Chard
Chenpi (chinese tangerine bowl)
Chestnut puree
Chestnuts
Chicken Blood
Chicken egg
Chinese cabbage
Chrysanthemum blossom tea
Clementines
Coconut grated
Coconut meat
Coconut milk
Coix (seeds) YiYi Ren
Corn
Corn (fast polenta)
Corn (roasted)
Corn flour
Corn germ oil
Corn Grease (Polenta)
Corn starch
Crab
Cranberry
Cranberry

Cranberry juice
Cream (30% fat)
Cream sour 20%
Cream, sweet 30%
Creamer
Curd cheese 40%
Currant jam (black)
Currant juice (black)
Currants (black)
Currants (red)
Curry paste red
Deer's kidneys
Emmental cheese
Evening primrose oil
Fennel
Fish sauce
French beans
Fresh cheese with herbs
Freshwater crab
Gail plum
Gelatin white
Goat and sheep's blood
Goose egg
Gooseberry
Gorgonzola
Gouda cheese
Grapefruit (Pomelo)
Grapefruit dried peel
Grapefruit juice
Grapes white
Grass carp
Greengage
Ground
Ground caraway
Halibut (Flatfish)
Hokkaido pumpkin
Lamb bones
Lamb meat
Lamb shoulder
Lamb's lettuce
Lettuce
Lobster
Luo Han Guo fruit
Lychee
Mackerel
Malt
Maple syrup
Mare's milk
Margarine
Margarine (diet)
Mixed Pickles
Morel (black, dried)
Mulberry fruit
Mung bean

Mutton
Nectarine
Nori, purple seaweed, red algae
Oat flakes roasted
Oat fusion (baby food)
Oat meal
Oat milk
Olives
Orange dried peel
Orange peel
Oyster mushroom
Parmesan
Passion fruit
Peanut oil
Pear
Pearl barley
Pepper (ground)
Pepper Cayenne
Pepper white (ground)
Peppercorns
Peppermint
Peppermint tea
Pepperoni
Pepperoni, red, pitted, halved
Pepperoni, yellow, pitted, halved
Peppers
Peppers (rose peppers)
Peppers (sweet)
Pickle
Pineapple juice without sugar
Plums
Pork heart
Pork liver
Pork meat
processed cheese 30%
Pudding powder vanilla
Pumpkin seed oil
Rabbit
Rabbit (wild)
Rabbit liver
Radish
Red berry (without sugar)
Reishi mushroom
Rice (fragrance)
Rice (Gaoliang / Sorghum)
Rice Basmati
Rice flour
Rice long grain rice
Rice malt
Rice noodles

Rice round grain
Rice starch
Rice sticky
Rice sweet
Rice variety any
Rose hip
Salmon
Salt
Shiitake, dried
Shrimp
Shrimps
Skim milk powder
Sour milk cheese 20%
Soy flour
Soy noodles
Soy sauce
Soy Tofu
Soy Tofu smoked
Soybeans
Soybeans, blacks, fermented
Strawberries
Sugar brown
Sugar substitute (sweetener)
Sunflower oil
Tabasco
Tarragon (Estragon)
Tomato
Tomato juice
Tomato puree
Tonic Water
Topinambur
Trout (smoked)
Tuna
Vanilla
Vanilla pod
Vanilla powder
Vinegar (Apple vinegar)
Vinegar (Red wine vinegar)
Vinegar Aceto Balsamico
Vinegar Aceto Balsamico white
Wakame
Walnuts
Walnuts roasted
Watermelon
Wax gourd
Wheat/Rye/Gray-black bread with yeast
Whole grain bread
Wholemeal flour
Wild strawberries
Zucchini

10.4 Do not use contra-acting foods

Acerola fruit nectar or powder

Almond

Almond marzipan
Almond puree
Apple (sweet)
Apple juice (natural cloudy)
Apple puree
Apricot dried
Apricot jam
Apricot nectar
Apricots
Apricots juice
Balm
Barley malt
Beef bone marrow
Beef kidney
Beer (alcohol-reduced)
Beer (Pils)
Beer (Top-fermented German dark beer)
Berry juice
Bitter Lemon
Bitter orange peel
Blackberry jam
Blueberry dried
Blueberry jam
Brown ale
Campari
Cashews
Champignon
Cherry
Cherry compote
Cherry juice
Chervil dried
Chicken egg white
Clarified butter
Coconut fat
Cola drink
Cola drink (low calorie)
Compote (fruits of the season)
Cooking oil
Cream sour 30%
Créme fraiche cheese
Cress
Crispbread
Crucian
Currant (black)
Currant (red)
Currant (white)
Currant jam (red)
Dandelion (young plants)
Dates dried
Dates red
Ducks egg
Eel
Eel smoked

Fernet Branca (herbal bitter liqueur)
Fig
Fig dried
Fructose (glucose)
Fruit mix juice
Fruit tea
Gentian root
Gentian root tea
Ginserg liqueur
Goose blood
Goose fat
Gourd
Grape juice red
Grape juice white
Grapes red
Green tea
Herbal tea mix
Honey
Honey wine (Met)
Horse meat
Kaki plum
Kiwi
Kombu seaweed (Saccharina japonica)
Kudzu
Ladyfingers
Lamb kidneys
Lamb liver
Lemon
Lemon juice
Lime
Lotus roots
Lychee in Preserved
Lychee liqueur
Lye rol
Mango
Mango juice
Martini
Mayonnaise 50%
Mayonnaise 80%
Mirabelle plum
Miso paste (soy bean paste)
Mold cheese
Muesli
Mulled Wine Spice
Multi-grain bread (gray bread)
Mutton
Nasturtium (nose-twister or nose-tweaker)
Noodles (wheat) with egg
Noodles (wheat, lasagne) with egg
Noodles (wheat, ribbon noodles) with egg
Noodles (wheat, spaghetti) with egg
Orange

Orange jam
Orange juice
Palm oil
Papaya
Peaches
Peaches (canned)
Peanut (roasted)
Peanut butter
Peanuts
Pear juice
Pineapple
Pineapple (from a can)
Plum
Plum dried
Pomegranate
Pork Bacon
Pork fat (lard)
Pork ham
Pork ham cooked
Pork ham smoked
Pork kidneys
Pork knuckle
Pork Lard
Pork marrow bones
Pork sausage (Bratwurst) Pork skin
Pork/beef sausage (smoked)
Prosecco
Puff pastry
Pumpernickel (dark bread)
Pumpkin seeds
Quince
Raisins
Raspberry jam
Red wine
Rhubarb
Rucola
Rum
Rusk
Sage
Sake
Salsify
Sauerkraut (cutted cabbage fermented)

Shark
Sherry (whine)
Sour cherries
Sourdough
Spirit
Strawberry jam
Strawberry Juice
Sugar - icing sugar
Sugar candy white
Sugar cane sugar
Sugar fructose - fruit sugar
Sugar glucose - grapes sugar
Sugar Milk Sugar
Sugar molasses
Sugar palm sugar
Sugar white
Tangerine
Toast bread (whole grain)
Tomato dried
Tomato paste
Turkey ham
Vanilla sugar natural
Vegetable juice
Wheat
Wheat beer
Wheat bran
Wheat bulgur
Wheat flakes
Wheat flatbread/pita bread
Wheat flour
Wheat flour whole grain
Wheat semolina
Wheat semolina for children
White bread (baguette)
White bread (pretzel sticks)
White bread (roll)
White bread (wheat bread)
White breadcrumbs
White dumpling bread (wheat bread cut
into White wine
Wormwood
Yoghurt vanilla

11 Herbs and their effects

11.1 Basil

thermal effect: warm
taste: spicy, bitter
Dries out, leads down. Tonifies Yang and Qi, dissolves mucus-cold,
eliminates wind-cold.
It has a beneficial effect on flatulence and nausea, relaxing and soothing.
Good to fight emphysema, bronchitis, whooping cough, high blood
pressure, headache, mouth odor, warts, hiccup, gout, migraine.

11.2 Mugwort

thermal effect: warm
taste: bitter, spicy
Regulates and nourishes bleeding, warms the inside, eliminates wind-
cold, eliminates parasites, eliminates heat, wetness, regulates and moves
Qi.
Reduces bleeding, alleviates pain. In the kitchen, mugwort is used as a
spice for fat food. Since it contains many bitter
substances, it boosts fat burning and promotes digestion.

11.3 Savory

thermal effect: warm
taste: bitter
Tonifies kidney yang, heart qi, stomach and spleen qi and warms the
middle, moves the liver qi and blood, releases mucous and cold from the
lungs, opens the surface, induces wind-cold.
Stomach-strengthening, soothing and appetizing. Ideal for prevent colds,
strengthens the immune system. In case of incontinence or nocturnal
wetting (not for children), put the beans in liquor for libido.

11.4 Coriander

thermal effect: warm
taste: spicy
Driving sweat, reducing wind, draining moisture, tonifying and regulating
qi, eliminating wind-cold.
The essential oils are appetizing, digestive, cramping and soothing in
stomach and intestinal disorders.

11.5 Herbs various

thermal effect: taste:
Stimulates appetite. Effect different.
Appetizing, lots of trace elements and vitamins.

11.6 Chives

thermal effect: warm
taste: spicy
Directs upward. Tonifies blood, kidney Yang and Qi. Dissolves moisture.
Bactericide, prevents cancer, strengthens gastric juice production,
promotes digestion and blood circulation, promotes
growth, triggers stagnation.

11.7 Lovage

thermal effect: warm
taste: spicy, bitter
Reduces inner wind and moisture, dissolves stagnation, directs upward,
warms Yang, regulates and moves Qi, warms inside, dissolves mucus-
cold, eliminates wind-cold.
Stimulates digestion, reduces pain. Extracts of the root are used to flush
out urinary tract infections and prevent kidney gravel.

11.8 Parsley

thermal effect: warm
taste: bitter
Nourishes blood and liver, harmonizes liver and spleen, strengthens
eyesight, preserves juices, contracts. Dissolves moisture and warms
Yang.
Stimulates liver function, detoxifies. Forces urinating. Relieves flatulence.
Digestive and menstrual stimulating, birth-accelerating, memory-
enhancing, blood-purifying, skin-smoothing.

11.9 Rosemary

thermal effect: warm
taste: bitter
Dries out, leads down. Strengthens the heart, lungs and spleen qi,
strengthens liver blood. Strengthens heart-Yin. Expels spleen heat / cold
moisture. Strengthens spleen and kidney yang.
Promotes digestion, relieves bloating, strengthens lung, spleen and

kidney. Affects the circulation and nerves. Appetizing. Baths help to fight circulatory disorders as well as with gout and rheumatism.

11.10   Black caraway

thermal effect: warm
taste: spicy, sweet
Dissolve / transform moisture, tonifyes Yang and Qi, moves blood, suppresses inner wind.
Detoxifying, immunoregulatory. In addition, the oil should stimulate the formation of bone marrow cells and generally protect body cells from viruses.

11.11   Tea mixture uric acid lowering

Uric acid-lowering.
Mix from the pharmacy or drugstore:
2 parts birch leaves, 1 part of broom, 1 part of stinging nettle, 3 parts of the chopping piece, 1 part of goldenrod.

11.12   Thyme dried

thermal effect: warm
taste: bitter
Strengthens the lungs and spleen. Clears wind-cold, dissolves slime-cold, tones qi, soothes Shen / Spirit.
Disinfecting. It stimulates the blood circulation, increases the appetite and helps to digest fat meat better. Strengthens lungs and spleen (TCM).

11.13   Yam root, yam root tuber

thermal effect: neutral
taste: sweet
Tonifies Yin, Yang and Qi, reduces inner wind, dissolves wetness, warms Yang.
Solves cramps (in the gastrointestinal tract). Digestive through increased bile production. Anti-inflammatory in rheumatic diseases.
Mucolytic agent for coughing. Relief of menopausal symptoms.

12 Basics of Nutrition

The basic principles of nutrition described herein are general recommendations. They are not aimed at a specific form of therapy. Recommendations concerning a therapy have priority.

12.1 Nutrition

Regular meals in a relaxed atmosphere. A warm breakfast is considered a good start into the day.
The main meals ought to be taken for lunch – supper in the early evening. Pay attention to feeling hungry or sated: don't eat too much nor remain hungry is the rule
Prepare the meals freshly from natural, regional products. Frozen, heat-conserved, industrially prepared or foodstuffs cooked in the microwave oven are rejected.
Choice of foodstuffs according to the season: more cooling food in summer, more warming food in winter.
Eat cooked food at least twice a day. Food and drinks ought to be lukewarm, never ice-cold or hot.
Raw vegetables, briefly cooked vegetables, freshly squeezed juices and mineral water are not recommended. Milk and dairy products are only included in the diet if they don't cause problems. Don't use therapeutic recipes over a longer period without consulting your doctor or therapist.

Varied food
Enjoy the diversity of foodstuffs. Characteristics of a balanced nutrition are variety, suitable combination and a balanced quantity of rich and low energy foodstuffs (on one hand avoiding undersupply with essential nutrients and on the other hand to take to many undesirable substances).

A lot of Cereal Products - and Potatoes
Bread, pasta, rice, cereal flakes (best wholemeal) as well as potatoes contain almost no fat, but many vitamins, mineral nutrients, trace elements, roughage and secondary plant substances. These foodstuffs ought to be taken with low-fat side dishes.

Vegetables and Fruit – „Take Five" every day ... 5 portions of vegetables and fruit a day, as fresh as possible, briefly cooked, or maybe one portion as a juice – ideal as a side dish to every meal as well as snack between meals: Thus a lot of vitamins, mineral nutrients as well as roughage and secondary plant substances

Daily milk and dairy products

Milk and Dairy Products every Day, once or twice per Week Fish; meat, sausages as well as eggs moderately. These foodstuffs contain valuable nutrients like calcium in the milk, iodine selenium and omega-3 fat acids in saltwater fish. Meat is favorable due to its high content of disposable iron and the vitamins B1, B6 and B12. Quantities of 300 – 600 g meat and sausage per week are sufficient. Prefer low-fat products, especially in meat- and dairy products.

Low-fat and fatty Foodstuffs
Fat supplies us with essential fat acids and fatty foodstuffs contain also fat-soluble vitamins. Fat is high in energy; therefore much fat in the food may cause overweight, possibly also cancer. Too many saturated fat acids may further a tendency for cardio-vascular diseases in the long term. Prefer vegetable oils and fats (e.g. rapeseed-, olive-, soya-oils and solid fats produced therefrom). Beware of invisible fat in meat- and dairy products, pastry and sweets as well as in fast-food and convenience foods. 70 – 90 g fat per day is sufficient.

Moderately Sugar and Salt
Take sugar and foods/drinks containing various kinds of sugar (e.g. glucose syrup) only occasionally. Use herbs and spices as well as a little salt creatively. Prefer salt containing iodine.

Plenty of Liquids
Water is absolutely essential. Drink 1-2 l liquids every day. Prefer water (with or without gas) and other low-calorie drinks. Alcoholic drinks should not be taken.

Tasty Dishes, carefully cooked
Cook the meals with as low temperatures and as short as possible, using little water and fat – this preserves the original taste, keeps the nutrients intact and prevents the production of harmful compounds.

Take time and enjoy the food
Take your Time and enjoy your Food
Eating consciously helps to eat right. The eye enjoys food, too. It's fun, invites to enjoy varied dishes and stimulates the feeling of satiety.

Watch your Weight and stay in Motion
A balanced diet and a lot of exercise and sport (30 – 60 min/day) are a healthy combination. The right weight furthers well-being and health. Thermals, directional effectiveness, digestive power
There are various criteria for judging the effectiveness of herbs and

foodstuffs.

The use of certain herbs and ingredients is based on observations of the effects on the body which these foodstuffs, herbs and spices show after having eaten them. The medical science has developed following system: Every ingredient or herb has a directional effectiveness. Furthermore, there are herbs which have a special effect on certain organs.

The basic condition for a healthy metabolism is to obtain sufficient energy from food and that the digestive process doesn't use too much energy. An easily digestible meal makes content and sated, doesn't cause flatulence and fatigue after the meal. The perfect spices increase the healthiness of our meals. Very often, just small doses of herbs and spices will suffice. They are not used to make us sated, but to help our digestive organs to digest the food.

12.2 Recipes

The recipes list the ingredients to be used and the cooking instructions show how the dish is prepared. The list of ingredients shows the concerned quantities as well as the relevance for the therapy. If you find „less than mentioned", try to comply or find an alternative from the „list of recommended foodstuffs". Mostly it shall result just in a small change of taste when you simply avoid this ingredient.

Mild cooking methods: boiling, stewing, poaching, steaming
Strong cooking methods: barbecuing, roasting, frying, smoking
Balanced cooking methods: deep-frying, baking brick
Deep-freezing and warming in the microwave oven should be avoided (denaturalization).

12.3 Foodstuffs

Foodstuffs have an effect on body and soul like medicinal herbs, only a very much milder one. Dietary advice is mainly based on regional foodstuffs. The knowledge about the effects of each foodstuff and the knowledge, when which foodstuff shall be used, is based on the orthodox school of medicine. Use ecologic-organic products, if possible. As everything should be cooked for a long time due to a better digestability and very rarely eaten raw, the food agrees with everyone.

The classification of the foodstuffs according to their effect on the body is the basis in order to achieve a harmonious status of health.

Dietary advisors do not recommend certain foodstuffs for everyone. The individual diet is tailor-made for the individual constitution.

Buy only fresh and ripe fruit and vegetables. You ought to leave unripe fruit and vegetables and such with brown spots and wilted leaves behind in the market. In this case take deep-frozen goods (never ready-to-serve dishes!). Fruit and vegetables are deep-frozen immediately after harvesting and often contain more vitamins and minerals than the goods from the vegetable shelf. Whereas conserved or tinned goods contain very much less biological substances. Also, salt, sugar and others are mostly added to the latter. Never leave the foodstuffs in the water after washing them to avoid that many vital substances get drowned. Clean salads, fruit and vegetables immediately before serving.

Please make sure of the hygienic processing of foodstuffs. Clean your salads, fruit and vegetables carefully. When cooking with meat, prepare all ingredients first and then process the meat products. Clean the worktop and tools very carefully. Wooden surfaces ought to be treated with a mild disinfectant regularly in order to reduce germination. Store fruit and vegetables separately, if possible. Harvested fruit and vegetables are still alive and emit e.g. ethylene gas, which makes other products ripen and age faster. Keep meat and fish in the closed packaging or store them in the fridge in closed containers.

12.4 Herbs

There are some basic rules for storing medicinal herbs. On principle, herbs must be protected from direct sunlight, humidity and heat.

Containers for the storage of herbs may be glasses, ceramic jars and even plastic containers. However, plastic is a rather unsuitable material and should only be a short-term solution. In case of glass containers, use a dark material.

Medicinal herbs cannot be kept for any long period. The shelf life of herbs is limited. However, it can be prolonged with suitable storage. The place should be dark, rather cool and absolutely dry. A wooden medicine cabinet, placed not directly next to a source of heat, would be ideal. Never buy large quantities of herbs so as not to have to throw them away. Label the container with the name of the herb and the date of harvesting or processing.

13 Other dietic-books

The following syndromes of dietetics, TCM or for a therapy supplement for cancer are available.

Dietetics
E001. Nutrition of the infant - baby food
E002. Nutrition during lactation
E003. Nutrition in old age
E004. Nutrition of children and adolescents
E005. Nutrition of athletes
E006. Light weight
E007. Pregnancy
E008. Full food

Protein and electrolyte - kidneys
E009. (hemodialysis) dialysis treatment
E010. Acute renal failure
E011. Chronic renal insufficiency
E012. Nephrotic syndrome
E013. Kidney stones (nephrolithiasis)

Gastrointestinal tract - pancreas
E014. Acute pancreatitis (inflammation of the pancreas)
E015. Chronic pancreatitis (inflammation of the pancreas)

Gastrointestinal tract - small intestine and large intestine
E016. Acute obstipation (constipation)
E017. Chronic obstipation (constipation)
E018. Colon irritabile
E019. Diverticulitis
E020. Acquired lactose intolerance (lactose malabsorption)
E021. Fructose malabsorption
E022. Glutensensitive enteropathy (celiac disease)
E023. Colectomy
E024. Short Bowel Syndrome

Gastrointestinal tract - liver, gallbladder, bile ducts
E025. Acute and chronic hepatitis (inflammation of the liver)
E026. Cholelithiasis (bile stones)
E027. fatty liver
E028. cirrhosis

Gastrointestinal tract - Stomach and duodenal intestine
E029. Acute gastritis
E030. Chronic gastritis
E031. Stomach bleeding
E032. Ulcus ventriculi and duodenal ulcer
E033. Condition after gastric surgery

Gastrointestinal tract - oral cavity and esophagus

E034. Stomatitis
E035. Esophageal carcinoma (esophageal cancer)
E036. Refluosophagitis (heartburn)

Special diseases
E037. Phenylketonuria (PKU)
E038. Rheumatic joint diseases

E039. **Metabolism** Obesity (overweight)
E040. Diabetes mellitus
E041. Eating disorders (underweight)

Fat metabolism
E042. Hypercholesterolaemia (increased cholesterol level)
E043. Hepatic Encephalopathy

Heart and circulation
E044. Arteriosclerosis (arterial calcification)
E045. Heart insufficiency
E046. Hypertension
E047. Hyperuricaemia and gout

E048. **Changed nutrient requirements** In case of fever
E049. For malignant diseases
E050. After burns
E051. Radiation and chemotherapy

E100. **CANCER** Pancreatic cancer
E101. Bladder cancer
E102. Blood cancer (leukemia)
E103. Breast cancer
E104. Colorectal cancer
E105. Gastric cancer
E106. Kidney cancer
E107. Esophageal cancer

E200. **TCM** Bladder - moisture heat in the bladder Bladder - moisture and cold in the bladder Bladder - emptiness and cold in the bladder
E201. Large intestine - external cold affects the large intestine Large intestine - moisture heat in the large intestine
E202. Large intestine - heat blocks the intestine II acute
E203. Large intestine - dryness of the colon
E204. Large intestine - Yang deficiency (cold)
E205. Heart - Blood insufficiency
E206. Heart - Blood stagnation
E207. Heart - Fire
E208. Heart - Hot mucus clogs the heart pores
E209. Heart - Cold mucus clogs the heart pores
E210. Heart - Qi deficiency
E211. Heart - Yang deficiency
E212. Heart - Yin deficiency
E213. Liver - Ascending Liver Yang
E214. Liver - Blood deficiency
E215. Liver - Blood stagnation

E216. Liver - Moisture heat in liver and gall bladder Liver - Fire
E217. Liver - Gall bladder Qi-Empty Liver - Cold in the liver meridian
E218. Liver - Qi stagnation Liver - Wind Liver - Wind with ascending liver Yang
E219. Liver - Wind with blood anemic
E220. Liver - Wind with extreme heat
E221. Lung - Qi deficiency Lung - Mucus-moisture in the lungs
E222. Lung - Mucus-heat in the lungs
E223. Lung - Mucus-cold in the lungs
E224. Lung - Dryness of the lungs
E225. Lung - Wind-heat attacks the lungs
E226. Lung - Wind-cold affects the lungs
E227. Lung - Yin deficiency
E228. Stomach - Bloodstagnation Stomach - Fire
E229. Stomach - Cold with liquid
E230. Stomach - Nutrition stagnation
E231. Stomach - Qi deficiency
E232. Stomach - Rebellious Qi
E233. Stomach - Yin Emptiness
E234. Spleen - Heat and moisture attack the spleen
E235. Spleen - Coldness and moisture affects the spleen
E236. Spleen - Qi deficiency
E237. Spleen - Qi deficiency + Declining spleen Qi
E238. Spleen - Qi deficiency + spleen does not control the blood
E239. Spleen - Yang deficiency
E240. Kidney - Heart and kidney no longer communicate
E241. Kidney - Jing deficiency
E242. Kidney - Kidneys cannot receive the Qi
E243. Kidney - Qi is not stable
E244. Kidney - Yang deficiency
E245. Kidney - Yin deficiency

For further information visit di-book.com.

14 EBNS - Software for nutritional counseling

The main task of the database is to create personalized nutritional advice for each patient individually. The database was developed for Dietetics and Traditional Chinese Medicine.
The Database supports training and advices in the daily work routine.

The computer program provides lists of recipes, ingredients and herbs, which are given to the client. individually adjustable according to patient's request from whole food to vegetarians (lacto, ovo, ...). For every register there is an information sheet which can be given to the client. All texts can be individually designed.

The syndromes can be combined and result in an intersection of the recommended recipes and ingredients. The automated diagnosis for the TCM enables you to check your experience during the training as well as to confirm your diagnosis in the working day. You select several predefined symptoms and have the program automatically display the relevant syndromes.

How to work with the database:
Select the patient / client, select one or more of the syndromes you diagnosed and print the folder.

You can change all values, create new symptoms or syndromes, develop recipes, change or adapt ingredients and herbs to your findings. In simple client management, all relevant data about the person is stored. You get an overview of the past diagnoses and the development of the course of the disease.

As a consultant you save a lot of time when you print out the recipe, food and herbal lists for the recognized syndromes and give them to the clients. You can use this time for a personal conversation. With the database, dieticians and nutritionists can view the nutrients and trace elements for each recipe and develop recipes for syndromes even with suggested ingredients.

All recipe and grocery lists can also be ordered from me as a combination of several diseases. I wish all readers good luck, health and happiness in life.
More information can be found at www.ebns.at.
Volunteer: www.krebsinfo.at
Josef Miligui